Praise for
Reimagining the Revolution

"*Reimagining the Revolution* is a deeply personal, compellingly passionate, and surprisingly comprehensive take on the horrid state of the American justice system. It is also quite literally an invitation to a revolution. Lehman-Ewing wants nothing less than the total elimination of our current system of incarceration and justice and its replacement with something both effective and humane. As she focuses on an array of ideas around race and justice, Lehman-Ewing presents vignettes from assorted lives—many interrupted by incarceration—that take us beyond the superficial stereotypes that serve as justification for the status quo. In arguing for the abolition of the current system, she advocates a radical rethinking of virtually every commonly held view about the value and actual practice of incarceration. Along the way, she reminds us that the 13th Amendment did not really end slavery and that vengeance is a poor excuse for irrational policies. Whether you agree with her revolutionary solution or not, you will almost certainly find her key arguments impossible to ignore."

—**ELLIS COSE,** author of *The Short Life and Curious Death of Free Speech in America* and *Race and Reckoning*

"*Reimagining the Revolution* is both a call to action and a series of road maps, showing readers how those most impacted by prisons and policing are creating a world in which both are rendered obsolete. Paula Lehman-Ewing invites us to see abolition not as a far-off goal, but as living practices and concrete programs that we can incorporate into our daily lives."

—**VICTORIA LAW,** journalist, coauthor of *Prison By Any Other Name* and author of *"Prisons Make Us Safer": And 20 Other Myths About Mass Incarceration*

"A timely and compelling exploration into the heart of contemporary social justice movements. Inspired by past and present events, Lehman-Ewing guides readers through the nuanced landscape of criminal justice reform and the profound racial reckoning that continues to shape our world. With a keen eye for dynamic storytelling, she introduces us to the courageous individuals at the forefront of change, providing a vivid tapestry of their journeys and contributions.

This book not only sheds light on the urgent need for societal transformation but also serves as a practical guide for those seeking to actively engage in the pursuit of justice. Lehman-Ewing's work is a testament to the power of storytelling in inspiring meaningful action. *Reimagining the Revolution* is an indispensable resource for anyone passionate about creating a more just and equitable world. A must-read that challenges, enlightens, and empowers."

—**JASON MASINO,** author of *Sinner's Prayer*

"In this personal exploration of today's abolition movement, Paula Lehman-Ewing takes the reader around the United States—the most incarcerated nation in human history—to reveal the creative and profound actions abolitionists are taking to make their communities safer and more free. *Reimagining the Revolution* provides vibrant and intimate portraits of people directly impacted by America's policies of mass incarceration, and shows how their work promises to change the world via concrete and pragmatic steps toward abolition."

—**PIPER KERMAN,** author of *Orange Is the New Black*

REIMAGINING
THE
REVOLUTION

REIMAGINING THE REVOLUTION

FOUR STORIES OF ABOLITION, AUTONOMY, AND FORGING NEW PATHS IN THE MODERN CIVIL RIGHTS MOVEMENT

PAULA LEHMAN-EWING

FOREWORD BY DR. ILYASAH SHABAZZ

North Atlantic Books
Huichin, unceded Ohlone land
Berkeley, California

Published by
North Atlantic Books
Huichin, unceded Ohlone land
Berkeley, California

Cover art and design by Jason Arias
Book design by Happenstance Type-O-Rama

Printed in the United States of America

Reimagining the Revolution: Four Stories of Abolition, Autonomy, and Forging New Paths in the Modern Civil Rights Movement is sponsored and published by North Atlantic Books, an educational nonprofit based in the unceded Ohlone land Huichin (Berkeley, CA) that collaborates with partners to develop cross-cultural perspectives; nurture holistic views of art, science, the humanities, and healing; and seed personal and global transformation by publishing work on the relationship of body, spirit, and nature.

North Atlantic Books's publications are distributed to the US trade and internationally by Penguin Random House Publisher Services. For further information, visit our website at www.northatlanticbooks.com.

Library of Congress Cataloging-in-Publication Data
Names: Lehman-Ewing, Paula, author.
Title: Reimagining the revolution : four stories of abolition, autonomy, and forging new paths in the modern civil rights movement / Paula Lehman-Ewing.
Description: Berkeley, CA : North Atlantic Books, [2024] | Includes bibliographical references and index. | Summary: "Strategies for abolition and liberation from four activist groups of the modern civil rights movement"-- Provided by publisher.
Identifiers: LCCN 2023057126 (print) | LCCN 2023057127 (ebook) | ISBN 9798889840794 (trade paperback) | ISBN 9798889840800 (ebook)
Subjects: LCSH: Discrimination in criminal justice administration--United States. | Racism--United States. | Civil rights--United States. | Equality--United States.
Classification: LCC HV9950 .L45 2024 (print) | LCC HV9950 (ebook) | DDC 323.173--dc23/eng/20240108
LC record available at https://lccn.loc.gov/2023057126
LC ebook record available at https://lccn.loc.gov/2023057127

1 2 3 4 5 6 7 8 9 KPC 29 28 27 26 25 24

Dedicated to my children:
May you strive to make
the world a better place.

Contents

Foreword by Dr. Ilyasah Shabazz   *xi*
Author's Note: About the Artists   *xv*
Preface   *xxvii*

1 The Way We Move   1

2 Systems of Oppression   17

3 Reimagining Communities: Ivan Kilgore,
United Black Family Scholarship Foundation   33

4 Reimagining Justice: Critical Resistance   57

5 Reimagining Capitalism: Greenwood   79

6 Reimagining Infrastructure: The Autonomous
Infrastructure Mission (AIM)   101

7 Conclusion: Beyond Freedom   123

Glossary   *143*
Acknowledgments   *153*
Notes   *157*
Index   *171*
About the Author   *179*

Foreword

by Dr. Ilyasah Shabazz

February 21, 2025 will mark the sixtieth anniversary of my father's political assassination. Sixty years ago, Malcolm X became a martyr for the millions to whom he dedicated his life. The gravitas of the name Malcolm X carries the same weight today as it did when my father met with global leaders and revolutionaries about liberty, justice, and the oneness of humanity. I worry, however, that the years have not been as kind to him as he was to us. Perhaps in our lifetime, the reader will learn just why his story was so inaccurately portrayed and why his message was so misconstrued.

The most devastating mischaracterization of Malcolm X is that he was a violent man. While the "radical" moniker may not carry the same weight as it did in my father's heyday, the mere invocation of "by any means necessary" has often been used to undermine his mission to liberate oppressed people the world over from the systemic oppressor.

Malcolm X first used the phrase "by any means necessary" in a speech given at the founding rally of the Organization of Afro-American Unity: "We declare our right on this earth to be a man," he said. "To be a human being, to be respected as a human being, to be given the rights of a human being in this society, on this earth, on this day, which we intend to bring into existence by any means necessary."

Since that oration, the phrase has been used to pit my father against the nonviolence of Dr. Martin Luther King Jr. when, in fact, they both shared the same goal: the elimination of systemic oppression. My mother, Dr. Betty Shabazz, once said that "by any means necessary" is not a violent statement but rather a "comprehensive" one. My father preached self-assurance, self-determination, and, if necessary, self-defense. Achieving humanity, however, should not require defending. Humanity is ordained by God.

After publishing my first book, *Growing Up X,* I felt the need to defend my parents for how I was raised—the extracurricular activities I participated in and the private schools and summer camps my sisters and I attended where we were among the few Blacks—and my father's legacy, until someone told me I never have to defend my father. All I have to do is share the beauty of Malcolm, the beauty he gave the world when he spoke about his belief in humanity and the oneness of all people, and the beauty that he gave to his wife and six daughters. Among my favorite speeches are his Message to the Grass Roots, his Letter from Has, and his remarks at Oxford University. There, you see him as a man who loves—who loves humanity, who loves truth, and who loves the power of education. It is this profound love that was truly revolutionary.

The Malcolm X & Dr. Betty Shabazz Memorial and Educational Center in New York City gathers people from all walks of life together to continue his revolutionary legacy of collective love and liberation. Located in the Audubon Ballroom, the historic site of my father's martyrdom, the center incubates social, racial, and global justice movements. More than merely memorializing the martyrdom of Malcolm X and the educational vision of Dr. Betty Shabazz, the center is also a gathering place for community organizers and educators who are training the next generation of leaders in the movement for racial equity and global justice.

I appeal to your humanity to love deeply and to move forward together to heal the wounds of corruption and oppression. The people you will meet in this book embrace this philosophy and embody the desperation that Malcolm X captured in his *"by any means necessary"* sermons. These fellow brothers and sisters are willing to start over and create anew, bringing about a world entirely different from what they have known. They are determined to step up as the next generation of liberators at a time when our efforts are under constant threat.

In an era marked by renewed struggles for justice and unrelenting calls for change, the legacy of Malcolm X reminds us of the importance of confronting deeply ingrained racial injustice. His unapologetic advocacy for the rights and empowerment of people of the African diaspora coupled with his uncompromising stance against systemic racism resonates deeply in contemporary discourse on racial inequality.

In the following pages, you will discover the impact of Malcolm X on contemporaries, such as Angela Davis and Ambassador Andrew Young, as well as on incarcerated freedom fighters Ivan Kilgore and Heshima Denham. These men and women embraced my father's call for action beyond protest and demonstration. My appeal to you is this: organize with strategy so that sixty years from now, we will not find ourselves in the same space as we were sixty years ago when my father was alive, simply insisting on liberty and justice for all.

Self Portrait by Scotty Scott aka Scott W. Smith

Author's Note: About the Artists

I think what draws me to art is the same thing that draws me to journalism: Ultimately, they are both an attempt to share untold stories in a way that people will take notice of.

I met my husband James in recovery. We were both trying our best to deal with everything life had to throw at us, and stay sober despite it all. At times it was exhausting: showing up in ways we hadn't before (usually because we were too inebriated to move); rushing off to meetings; putting out fires that arose from sparks ignited during a messier time. But other times it was boring. When it came to fun, we only knew one way, which had stopped being fun long before we stopped doing it.

This common experience among newly sober individuals translated very acutely to James, to the point that it made him jittery. His hands had primarily been used to move a drink from a bartop to his mouth for so long that they ached to go back to his old routine. At one point, his mother told him he used to doodle as a child when he was bored in school. Maybe he could try that.

James began to draw in charcoal. He did a self-portrait, a drawing of his mother with her dog, a classic car, and scenes from movies with captivating scoundrels, like Daniel Day-Lewis as William Cutting in *Gangs of New York*. Within a year, he had enough to display in a brief gallery run. We called the exhibit *See the Light in Black and White*.

I firmly believe that art saved my husband in these early years of sobriety, just as the art of writing saved me. As the actor Stella Adler once said, "Life beats down and crushes the soul, and art reminds you that you have one."

It is this soul-baring that has fostered my deep affection for and connections with incarcerated writers and artists. It is their willingness to open themselves up to a world that has closed them off that inspires the work I do and the friendships I've made with the men and women I've worked with behind prison walls.

These relationships stem primarily from my time as the newspaper editor for the grassroots organization All of Us or None. The group's onboarding process emphasized the importance of putting people most directly impacted by mass incarceration at the forefront of every policy initiative, demonstration, and call to action. I took that directive quite literally, making sure someone who was in prison owned the very front of the newspaper every month, with a full-page image of artwork by an incarcerated artist.

Over the years, various organizations and individuals have aggregated these works, not only because of the quantity of art being produced inside the prison system but their quality as well. Arts in Corrections, California Arts in Corrections, and the Justice Arts Coalition all run programs that provide space and materials for artists to create drawings, paintings, sketches, and sculptures, often with the artists' permission to display photographs of their completed work on the organization's website.

When I first started working on the paper, I would peruse these resources for potential cover art. I was immediately blown away by the skillfulness and the beauty in each piece. Even the more gritty or gory drawings were breathtaking in their own right. The psychological strength these artists had to possess to produce something so beautiful amid an environment so horrific had a profound impact on me. As life has continued to have its ups and downs, I have tried to find the beauty amid all of it.

On the first day in April 2020, I sent roughly 500 copies of the paper's first edition to individuals incarcerated in California, including the cover artist to whom I had written a note about his work and sent two extra copies. By the end of the month, I had a stack of mail postmarked by the California Department of Corrections and Rehabilitation. The envelopes were filled with pages and pages of handwritten letters on yellow legal pad paper. I read each one as best I could. Most were legible, but the overwhelming majority were penned by trauma-induced shaky hands. I also received a letter from the cover artist, graciously accepting my apology for printing his work without his direct permission (I had downloaded the image from one of the aforementioned sites) and thanking me for getting his work "over the prison walls." He had sent one of the extra copies to his mother, who was proud of a son the world had told her to disgrace. A warming experience for all three of us.

After the first wave of letters, a new one arrived, this batch packaged in much larger envelopes. They contained drawings in a variety of mediums: Some were simply doodles alongside poetry; others were more classical acrylic works from prisons where those supplies had been made available. I rarely had to pull from the web for cover art after that.

Two artists in particular stood out to me—Gerald Morgan and Scott Smith—which is why their work appears in this book. The following is an attempt to help you know them beyond the "prisoner" label on their jumpsuits and to provide some context about the images in this book. I also profile Carnell Hunnicutt, an artist who created a graphic novel version of *Race to Incarcerate* during his incarceration. These artists' work embodies what French sculptor Auguste Rodin articulated as the key elements of art: "to be moved, to love, to hope, to tremble, to live."

*"I want to touch people with my art. I want them to say,
'he feels deeply, he feels tenderly.'"*
—VINCENT VAN GOGH

Gerald Morgan

 Gerald Morgan's *Doing Time* painting, which precedes chapter 6, appeared on the June 2020 cover of All of Us or None's newspaper, published a week after police officers killed George Floyd in Minneapolis. It still strikes me here, but the original is truly devastating, shaded with midnight blues, crafted with delicate brush strokes that create the various brown tones that contour the main figure.

After receiving the June paper and my note, Gerald wrote to me that the experience of seeing his art used in such a manner brought him a glimmer of light during a "dark time" in his life. At that point Gerald had been incarcerated for twenty years. He had been locked down in his cell for months due to the pandemic and denied access to the San Quentin art studio that had served as a saving grace for him throughout the years. It was lonely, and a haunting reminder of what it felt like to be new in prison again.

Gerald had been released by the time I finished *Reimagining the Revolution*. I was able to track him down through the Humans of San Quentin, a humanitarian nonprofit that proliferates the stories of individuals impacted by the criminal justice system. They had interviewed Gerald upon his release and passed along his information.[1] I was anxious to ask him about the piece that had moved me so greatly and had brought us together.

"I've seen that specific face in a number of individuals including myself," he told me when we finally connected. "Whenever we are doing time, we don't ever know what to expect from one day to the next. As far as the possibilities of paroling, that's always happening way outside the door. We have a deep, dark understanding of where we are and nothing is open to us except maybe a back door. The element of freedom is so far beyond."

It was a feeling that hit Gerald hard when he first entered the prison system in 1998. For the first two years, he said, he isolated, rarely leaving his cell for fear of what he might encounter in the general population. He had begun to feel "invisible," something he captured in *Anticipation*, which precedes this book's introductory chapter. *Anticipation* is a retelling of the faces he saw in the prison visiting room, anxious women in a strange place waiting with both excitement and apprehension. Sometimes, Gerald said, "they don't even see you."

The feelings of loneliness and fear were so acute in these early years that they crept up twenty-two years later, long after he'd already integrated himself with the men he was incarcerated with and developed friendships he holds to this day.

Most of these relationships were fostered in the art studio. As a child, Gerald had loved to draw, so he gravitated toward the studio. He met other artists I've worked with, such as Bruce Fowler, who taught him how to mix paints, and Isaiah Daniels, who instructed him on photorealism. The men in the studio became his "perimeter," the people he could feel comfortable around and relate to. They were his peers and teachers, and the studio was his sanctuary.

I asked him about this dichotomy—the life he lived in prison and the life he lived in the art studio—which he depicted in both the beauty and sadness of *Doing Time*.

"That's the only time when it *don't* feel like you're doing time," he said. "Beyond that front door to that art studio is prison, but when you come into that art studio and you're creating something or learning something, you don't think about what's going on beyond that door. You get a chance within the studio for your mind to be free as well as your body as you create."

Since his release in February 2023, Gerald has reunited with his family, including his sister, whose portrait introduces chapter 4. He bought a full-size easel and extra canvases and has started work on his next art project. He got a job working by Pier 39, a section of San Francisco's Fisherman's Wharf that is lined with high-end art galleries, but he says his inspiration is still drawn from the men he left behind across the Bay.

"My roots are still in the prison system. They got me through all that time, and those are the people I'm connected to, the people I still reach out to when I'm tossing around ideas."

"Art is the only way to run away without leaving home."
—TWYLA THARP

Carnell Hunnicutt Sr.

In the preface of this book, you'll read about Carnell Hunnicutt, a graphic artist who transformed Marc Mauer's *Race to Incarcerate* into a graphic novel. An "official" graphic novel was published by the New Press in 2013, but it was illustrated by established artist Sabrina Jones, supposedly, according to a presentation Marc gave, with a blessing from an incarcerated creator. The whole thing seemed shady, so I started looking for the original artist. "Carnell Hunnicutt," as he appeared briefly in Marc's introduction, was easy to find via a simple Google search. The top hit is a link to his aggregated work on the Real Cost of Prisons Project (www.realcostofprisons.org), a website that includes written work and comics by prisoners, a daily news blog focused on mass incarceration, and three comic books for purchase. The landing page for Carnell's work begins with a picture of him with RCPP founder Lois Ahrens, a brief copyright statement, and a note: "Great news! Carnell is free!!!"

After some internet sleuthing, I found out that Carnell had been freed from a supermax prison in Sommers, Connecticut, in March 2023 after twenty-nine years of incarceration. He had moved back home to Texas and reconnected with his family. I pinged him on Facebook and eventually we got on the phone.

I asked him about what went down with Marc, and if he'd conceded to having another artist run with his idea. Although Carnell was wounded by the interaction (as you'll read in the preface), he said that he faced many challenges as an incarcerated artist, namely access to supplies and retaliation from correctional officers.

"I wanted to tell my story through art because I was witnessing things as a prisoner that show how corrupt the Department of

Corrections and the whole system is," Carnell said. "I wanted to tell the story of what I was enduring and what I was witnessing during that time."

The Connecticut prison department put Carnell in and out of solitary confinement for a total of thirteen years. In isolation, Carnell started reading about politics, socialism, and capitalism. He read about Black liberation movement leaders like Malcolm X and Marcus Garvey. He read Michelle Alexander's *The New Jim Crow* and Mauer's *Race to Incarcerate*, creating comic book versions of each, once he could access pen, paper, and a decent source of light again. The first page of his version of *Race to Incarcerate* precedes chapter 2.

Every time Carnell would emerge from solitary, his drawings would become a little more political, a little more pointed at the injustices of the system that confined him. He took on issues like overcrowding, police violence, and guards' attacks on prisoners. He drew two non-comic images with colored pencils of a segregation cell and the prison's "recreation cage," a space boxed in by a fourteen-foot concrete wall and a steel cage roof—prisoners' only access to fresh air and sunlight.

Each illustration brought increasingly harsher consequences, which Carnell says he has nightmares about to this day. Once guards put him in four-point bed restraints and beat him. They put him on "pen restriction," not only removing his sole artistic tool but the instrument with which he could file an appeal against such action. When he was able to smuggle in ink cartridges, guards tried to break his hands.

These attempts had the opposite effect from their intent: Rather than break Carnell into submission, they fueled his artistic desire.

"A lot of my best work comes from the supermax. You're down 24/7; you have no contact with anyone; you're chained up when you come out, strip-searched when you leave, and antagonized by the guards. And you can't put your hands on them, so you need an outlet. My outlet was my art.

"I could use it to tell them off, make them laugh, or tell a story. I directed my anger into my artwork to keep me at peace."

Since his release, Carnell says, he hasn't had much time for drawing. He's reestablishing relationships with his children and family, working on getting his commercial driver's license, and adapting to a society that has changed dramatically in the thirty years since he last saw it. He does have plans, however, to aggregate his work, much of which he sent to his brother-in-law for safekeeping, and publish an anthology of the art that kept him at peace during his darkest hours.

> *"The aim of art is to represent not the outward appearance of things, but their inward significance."*
> —ARISTOTLE

Scott Smith

The most prolific contributor to the newspaper was Scott "Scotty Scott" Smith. He was featured in All of Us or None in September 2020 after he sent an ink and pencil drawing entitled *COVID Creature*.[2] It reminded me of a Ralph Steadman caricature from *Fear and Loathing in Las Vegas*. Crooked fingers hold a circular object detailed with a grid pattern over a misshapen face. I couldn't stop looking at it and was even more taken aback when I saw it was made with simple tools I had in.my desk pen holder.

I scanned the image and published it alongside a column about COVID inside prisons written by an incarcerated contributor. I sent three issues to Scotty with a personal note and a list of topics I planned to cover in the months ahead. Within weeks, he sent a drawing for the October "Election Issue," an image drawn in a completely different style. It is full color, and while still a bit cartoonish, not at all abstract like the COVID creature. It portrays a man in an orange hoodie and baggy jeans with a backpack, arms crossed, and eyes covered by sunglasses. He stands between two signs, one yellow that reads "It's Not Too Late . . . So VOTE And . . ." and a stop sign that reads "Stop Hate."

I used Scotty's drawings in so many consecutive issues that I had to hold off for a couple of months to ensure other artists were being recognized. But then he sent me *Bigger Than Life*, a black-ink portrait of Rep. John Lewis. Scotty's delicate pen strokes depicted Lewis's stoic yet booming presence, his eyes focused and determined above carefully shadowed cheekbones. After printing it in the March 2021 issue, I framed it and put money in Scotty's commissary account with the memo "fine art." Mounted above my desk as I write this, the drawing still moves me.

Our correspondence continued after I left All of Us or None. Scotty still contributes to the paper, and about a year after I left I saw his drawing *Not Feeling the Freedom*, which prefaces chapter 3, on the cover of another issue. It had also been published by Prison Journalism Project, a fairly new enterprise that mentors and features incarcerated writers and brings their work into the mainstream.

"The Statue of Liberty is supposed to symbolize freedom for all American people, but the statue is an imposter," Scotty wrote on the PJP website. "The only ones who are free in this country are the super-rich. They can do whatever they want and get away with it because money buys power. Everyone I know in prison is poor. Poverty is what causes crime—it's always been this way."[3]

Scotty still sends me incredible works of art, including the two other pieces featured in this book. The portrait of Dr. Martin Luther King Jr. that leads into chapter 5 is in a similar style to the John Lewis drawing hanging above my desk. *The World Right Now*, the acrylic that introduces chapter 7, has this inscription on the back: "It doesn't matter if one is black, white, red, or brown. We are all just bricks. We are all just the same inside. It is amazing to me most people don't get it. As Pink Floyd once sang, 'We are all just bricks in the wall.' It should go without saying black bricks matter and without them, the whole thing comes tumbling down."

I can't offer Scotty much of an exchange in the way of art—I have a hard enough time staying within the lines of my son's coloring books—but I do maintain a close relationship with him. We check in

regularly on a ViaPath Technologies–issued tablet, a recent technological advancement in prison communications that allows prisoners
to send digital correspondence and schedule video visits.

For most of our friendship, Scotty has been incarcerated in the
state prison in Corcoran, California. We have never spoken on the
phone, nor have we had any video visits. He tells me he's "grown old
in prison," that he's lost most of his teeth due to "things that happened in here," and requested I not include a photo of him in this
book. Instead, he sent me probably my favorite work of his to date,
Self Portrait, which precedes this note. To me it embodies everything
this book is about: the complex web of colors and shapes that define
our humanity, the array of perceptions our faces provoke in different
onlookers, and the demand and challenge to absorb every detail.

"I have realized in myself a sense of wanting fairness and prosperity for everyone in the world regardless of who they are, what their
creed and whatever the sexual preference, so long as it hurts no one
else," Scotty wrote in the note accompanying the portrait. "I feel deep
inside me a call to fight the Good fight for all people, however especially for my people, my fellow inmates and convicts, no matter what
kind of mistakes they have made."

In my mind, Scotty looks like a moving shadow, his features indiscern-
ible and his voice rendered mute. In the absence of physical attributes, I
am able to unearth what truly connects us. To me, he is his passion for
art. He is a person who can find beauty in both color and grayscale, who
uses whatever he has to make something great in the hopes that it will be
seen by even a single person on the outside. On the back of each drawing
he's sent is a note: "Use it if you want, or just enjoy it."

Of the three artists featured in this book, only Scotty remains in
prison. As he enters his second decade of incarceration, he only asks
one thing in return for his work: That you look at it, and that by seeing
it, he may be seen as well.

"There is no must in art because art is free."

—WASSILY KANDINSKY

Prison art, by its very nature, is revolutionary. Simply creating art in a system designed to deprive people of identity and beauty is a form of protest. It is an expression of freedom in a world of restrictions and cages. For many incarcerated individuals, this possession of their internal freedom to create is both what keeps them going and what makes their work so devastatingly beautiful.

I want to acknowledge Peter Merts, a photographer, whose portraits of Gerald's work and art from other California prisoners created a conduit between myself and the incarcerated artists I've met and been inspired by. Peter not only photographs these works of art in a professional way, but he also captures the joy and passion each artist experiences in creating them, with candid shots of different classes. This human element helps visitors of his website see these men and women as artists, not prisoners or faceless producers. I encourage you to visit PeterMerts.com to learn more about arts in the carceral setting.

Gerald, Carnell, and Scotty were compensated for their contributions to this book. Each one volunteered his work at first, but their generosity was denied for two important reasons. I relay them here in hopes that future collaborations become more equitable between artists who have experienced incarceration and those who are perhaps working with them for the first time.

The more obvious reason is hypocrisy. The following pages will dive into the dehumanization that occurs in the prison-industrial complex and the exploitation of prison labor. There can be no advocacy against slavery and involuntary servitude if we proliferate the very nature of these practices. While the use of "forced" labor may not be relevant here, the potential for exploitation—either intentional or by accident—is always present. "As far as I'm concerned, your days of working for nothing are done," I said to Gerald.

The second is artistry. I've paid Scotty for works I've never used in a newspaper or book because I consider his work valuable, and him an artist, and, as such, compensate him accordingly. The drawings in *Reimagining the Revolution* could easily go for six figures at some of the Pier 39 galleries Gerald walked by on his way to work, but context

is important. And while society may see the context of a gallery as
heightening the value of a piece of art, I see the context in which incarcerated works are designed as reason to elevate prison art to an even
higher level of worth. I see their boldness and their unwavering dedication to freedom as inspiring and awesome, in the biblical sense.
It's hard to put a price on that kind of context, but it's worth at least
throwing a few figures around.

Preface

When I started writing this book and interviewing the people it would include, I was often asked why. Why this topic? Why you?

It's a valid question. The struggle for racial equality is a long one, seemingly endless. It has required miles of footwork, a deluge of bloodshed, and years of endurance to withstand the ebb and flow of social consciousness, political dysfunction, and surges of white rage. Why would anyone who isn't tied to the movement by their cultural and sociopolitical identity ever volunteer to join?

My interest in struggles for liberation grew out of my understanding of collective humanity, informed by my Jewish ancestry. Early on in life, I connected far more with the human race than I did a white race. My Jewish grandparents were not considered "white"; neither were their Irish neighbors, although the descendants of these generations were. This informed me that race can be flexible. With near arbitrary parameters, the social construction that is race cannot possibly be an excuse to disengage from the struggle for liberation. So when asked why, my usual response is "Why wouldn't I?"

This book is my attempt to ensure that the atrocities humans inflict on each other—whether enslavement, genocide, or imprisonment— never fill another museum or warrant another memorial. If you see humanity as a connection to the human race, it is incumbent upon you to speak out against injustice inflicted upon your fellow human. Staying out of the fray will provide shelter for only so long. When they come for you, *your* justice will be sought by the people you fight for now.

Decisions

My journey into the revolution began when the grassroots organization All of Us or None hired me to write a newspaper amplifying the voices of currently and formerly incarcerated people. The majority of my career had been in journalism, but after covering the criminal legal system as a beat reporter, I felt a need to push for change in a less objective manner.

By May 2020 I had a pretty solid rhythm going with the paper. Every month I'd gather stories from traumatized individuals who had been seen as society's monsters and treated accordingly. I'd weave their pained statements into dense articles, connecting their present-day tribulations to distant court rulings and political pivots that could provide clues on how to target the next reform and prevent the next injustice. The articles were placed alongside statistical graphics, photographs of the organization's demonstrations, and intricate drawings made by incarcerated artists with colored pencils, watercolors, and ink pens. I'd pay a couple of editor friends out-of-pocket to put eyes on it, and finally, I'd print out each page on 11×17-inch paper to make "proofs"—a publishing term for hardcopy drafts laid out for review before the pages go to press.

Working from home due to the raging pandemic, I was spastically taping the June proofs to the living room wall when I received an alert about George Floyd's death in Minneapolis. The heavy printouts crashed onto the floor as I read about a man crying out for his mother, suffocated because of an untried counterfeit charge.

My husband and my son came into the room, the rustle of papers still settling from the tumble.

"What?" James asked, as our son gleefully wrapped one of the pages around his belly like a gym towel. James began to unwrap him with a gentle "Mommy needs that," but I quickly interjected.

"No, I don't. I need to rewrite everything."

The feature story planned for the June newspaper was about the existence of slavery in the US Constitution—as well as many state constitutions—and the moral and societal consequences of that. In examining the 13th Amendment's carve-out that preserved slavery—"Neither slavery nor involuntary servitude, except as a punishment for crime"—I had taken aim at the monetary greed fueling incarceration, explaining how the subsequent forced labor had created a multibillion-dollar-a-year system that lines the pockets of correctional staff and administrators, as well as corporate bigwigs looking to skimp on production costs.

But as I read more about the murder in Minneapolis, about the police officer, Derek Chauvin, who had knelt on Floyd's neck for almost nine minutes as he died, it struck me: The persistence of slavery in America could be attributed to something, if possible, even more sinister than greed. The reason why so many Black people are dehumanized by the law is that the men who designed those laws did so in a way that would ensure the people they captured and forced to build this country would never truly be able to call it home. Racism infiltrates law enforcement and criminal legal proceedings because America's original sins—colonialism, genocide, and slavery—have been solidified and carried forth in the country's foundational legal documents.

I sat down to rewrite the opening paragraph:

> If you're wondering how a police officer can dig his knee into the neck of a Black man, cut off his oxygen, and murder him on camera . . . the answer is not simply that racism still exists in this country. It is that the original system of racism in this country still exists in a very real and very legal way.[1]

The following week, the California chapters of All of Us or None had a virtual planning meeting to discuss how we'd demonstrate that instances of police brutality were not one-off anomalies by rogue officers. We wanted to highlight the multigenerational reinforcement of white supremacy that had influenced law enforcement training and protocols and led to this moment. In any other year, the decision would have been easy: Make signs and hit the streets. But there were a couple of problems with this model.

The nation was still grappling with the novel coronavirus, and the idea of standing shoulder-to-shoulder with countless strangers seemed risky. It was a calculated risk that many were still willing to take, but as formerly incarcerated individuals, the membership of All of Us or None was in a particularly high-risk category. Many of them were older, and years of unsanitary conditions, lack of sunlight, and subpar health care had taken their toll.

Simultaneously, the modern movement for civil rights was evolving. Many organizers were beginning to see that traditional ways of protesting had led to negligible gains. My old photojournalism professor, Ken Light, released a book with his wife, Melanie, that summer called *Picturing Resistance: Moments and Movements of Social Change from the 1950s to Today*; and to be honest, if it wasn't in chronological order, the movements it depicts would be almost indistinguishable. As you flip through, you begin to realize protests around justice and equality have looked pretty much the same over the last half century: fists raised in 1960s Birmingham, Alabama, and Ferguson, Missouri, in 2015; plumes of smoke blanketing the park outside the 1968 Democratic National Convention in Chicago and covering crowds in Kenosha, Wisconsin, in 2020.

What's worse is that most of these protests are about the same things: police brutality, disenfranchisement, and racist policies. Demonstrations had created a surplus of moving images, but the reforms enacted in their wake left room for racial injustice to evolve, rather than dissolve. Felony disenfranchisement laws combined with rising numbers of Black individuals being criminalized had undone most of the accomplishments of the Voting Rights Act of 1965. Despite the grotesque images of officers hosing down peaceful protestors at the height of the civil rights movement, the US Supreme Court introduced the *qualified immunity doctrine*, easing the amount of liability officers face after violent clashes with the public, in 1967 (Pierson v. Ray, 386 US 547). And while not explicitly racist in their terminology, sentencing laws have further served to criminalize and subjugate non-white denizens, as has the advent of "hot-spot policing."

In an attempt to break the cycle, ideas were beginning to percolate in the 2020s about new ways to rebel and reimagine the fight for racial justice—ideas that took these evolutions into account, and were becoming more strategic as they manifested into plans for social change.

Unfortunately, the Stop Killing Us protest, the demonstration we'd planned, did end up looking very much like previous protests. It featured signs—photographs of 600 men and women killed by police were printed on 20 × 24-inch poster boards. Some classic marching was even supposed to happen, but due to the pandemic and poor planning, not enough people showed up to have each photo elevated. Instead of the signs being held, they were displayed atop the Capitol's steps in Sacramento, creating a sort of morbid mosaic.

I sat on a bench with my mentor Ken Oliver, watching a typical protest unfold in a typical fashion. People chanted, impassioned speeches were made, and a few lawmakers emerged from the building to issue some generic support.

"This ain't gonna do it," Ken said passively.

A Search for Answers

Ken was right, and I hated that, especially when I'd been working overtime, spending my days and evenings reading about different ways people have been murdered by police. But while my knowledge of politics and criminality comes from learned experience—higher education, two decades in journalism, hundreds of interviews, countless books and papers—Ken's comes from learned *and lived* experience. As such, when it comes to the fight for liberation—a fight he's had to personally take on in his own life—he's often right.

Ken and I became friends after discovering our mutual passion for understanding how things work. We quickly disregarded the glaring differences that often cause passersby to double-take when a Black man and a white woman meet up for coffee or drinks. Although he's not wildly tall, Ken does cast a shadow on most acquaintances. His frame is broad, his dark eyes heavy with severity, and his voice deep and stoic. When we first met, he had been out of prison for almost a year and still had his "prison body," a bulky upper torso from a routine dictated by spatial limitations. In a full plank, he'd probably have a couple of feet between his extremities and the walls of his cell. This hardened physical appearance, remnants of a past life where it was required for survival, is juxtaposed with a generous heart, a love of learning, and a dedication to justice and self-discovery.

While my pursuit of answers got me into college, Ken's got him entangled with the state. For example, in 1997 he wanted to understand how a guilty plea in the criminal case against him would save him from a life behind bars should he exercise his 6th Amendment right to trial. Los Angeles County Judge Stephen E. O'Neil had agreed to remove a prior "strike" offense and sentence Ken to fourteen years, but Ken had to plead guilty right then and there.

"When you're talking 14 years versus the rest of your life, how long do you need, Mr. Oliver?" the judge said, per the court transcript. "You take it today or we go to trial."

Ken wanted to check in with his family, sleep on it, and weigh the pros and cons, as anyone would have done when making a decision that would change the course of his life. He was denied that opportunity, so he decided to take his chances with a jury. After a four-day trial, the judge sentenced Ken to two life sentences under California's new Three Strikes law, his penalty for inconveniencing the court.

While he was inside, Ken did what a lot of people in his position do: He started reading. He read books about criminal law and the mechanics of the criminal justice system. He studied the writings of Black revolutionary authors like James Baldwin, Frantz Fanon, and George Jackson. Again, his pursuit of knowledge was met with punishment: His possession of Jackson's work landed him in solitary confinement—guards insisted his interest in Jackson linked him to a prison gang and threw Ken into the security housing unit. He spent eight and a half years buried in a container beneath Pelican Bay State Prison, eventually joining others in a hunger strike to protest the cruelty of solitary. The strike helped settle litigation that ended indeterminate solitary confinement in the state. Ken was put back into the population, transferred, and, ultimately, released in 2019 under Proposition 57, which required parole consideration for "nonviolent felons" serving life sentences under the Three Strikes law.[2]

After spending twenty-three years and eight months inside, Ken walked out of prison and into the offices of Legal Services for Prisoners with Children, the fiscal sponsor of All of Us or None Oakland. A year later, when I met him, he had climbed the ranks to become the organization's policy director.

Between his experience and the carceral curriculum he designed for himself, Ken is the perfect sounding board for someone like me, someone with a little knowledge and a lot of questions. When I first started writing this book, I sent a draft proposal to some former colleagues for input. The draft included a statement that racial injustices and violations of civil liberties "are more prevalent today than at any other point in US history." When some white reviewers had responded with "You can't say that," I called Ken.

"Yeah, you can absolutely say that," he said matter-of-factly.

"But the images of American slavery, they're just horrific," I said, regurgitating the feedback I'd gotten. "Bodies covered in scar tissue from being whipped? People dying, malnourished in the fields?"

"I see those lashings in every Black man that's been shot in the back by the police. I see guys out there in Angola [State Prison in Louisiana], pickin' the same plantations as their ancestors."

As he usually does, Ken pointed me to a revolutionary writer to get educated. This time it was Frantz Fanon, a political philosopher born in colonial Martinique. In his book *Black Skin, White Masks*, Fanon wrote, "For the Black man there is only one destiny. And it is white."[3] In other words, the experience of Black people may look different at various points in time, but the oppression remains the same for those who do not assimilate into white culture. We can keep making changes to the current system, but as long as it fundamentally remains intact, there is only one outcome for the systematically oppressed: Accept the status quo. Otherwise, the consequences can be dire, even deadly.

The lesson from Ken and Fannon stuck with me, as did the dismal results of the Stop Killing Us protest in Sacramento, and the mirror images of past and present demonstrations. I began to rethink how we could move the needle, how we could redirect our path to progress, how we could reimagine the revolution.

Thus started the process of identifying the people with lived experiences who are not just trying to move differently, but aim differently. Rather than targeting areas of the current system for reform, they're focused on replacing the current system entirely. Their movements are wholly dependent on creative, outside-the-box thinking, informed by personal experiences. Their revolutions take on the way we develop communities, the prison system, the economy, and the infrastructure that dictates how our society functions. Together, we'll visit their base commands where conversations are being had about not just how to tear down these systems, but what to replace them with.

But Enough about Me

When I first wrote this book, I omitted myself completely. In workshopping some sample chapters, however, there was a natural curiosity about who I was and how I came to cross paths with the people in this book. To that end, there are some stories about my journey to and around the modern civil rights movement early on. But as we enter the heart of the book—the chapters profiling the movement architects—these personal anecdotes fade away. My voice appears as a guide throughout, but my goal is to amplify the voices of others, not speak for them or over them.

Consider me an access point, a conduit into worlds you may otherwise not be aware of or exposed to. I will be your eyes and ears in the rooms of revolution—but I do not presume to own the messages that emanate from them. The ideas, plans, and theories contained in this volume are presented through the lens of those most directly impacted by systems of oppression. All the conversations detailed here regarding those ideas were consensually held, and each person represented has agreed to be portrayed. It is their up-close and personal encounters with the systems they are in conflict with that have informed their solutions. It is their willingness to have their stories told that allowed this book to happen.

Glenn Martin, a formerly incarcerated activist you will meet in the chapter "Reimagining Communities," has a saying: "Those closest to the problem are closest to the solution and furthest from power and resources." My intention with this book is to amplify the stories of system-impacted individuals, so they may be heard and considered in places of power they may not otherwise have reached.

Ivan Kilgore, whose organization is profiled in the aforementioned chapter on community building, is currently serving a life sentence. During his twenty-plus years of incarceration, he has self-published four books: a social commentary on incarceration (*Domestic Genocide: The Institutionalization of Society*), a memoir (*Mayhem, Murder & Magnificence: A Memoir*), an urban novel (*King: The Early Years*), and an anthology (*My Comrades' Thoughts on Black Lives Matter: A Collection of Essays and Poems*). There's a reason why you're learning about him and his life from this book, not from one of the autobiographical writings he's penned himself. Oppressive systems deny voice to the oppressed, whether by voter disenfranchisement or by denial of access—access to publishers, to computers, and, by design, access to mainstream society.

Even self-proclaimed advocates struggle with the existing barriers to authentically amplify incarcerated voices. Marc Mauer, for example, spent thirty-three years compiling data on sentencing discrepancies and voter disenfranchisement. As the executive director of the Sentencing Project, Marc used this data to campaign for criminal justice reforms. He is also the author of *Race to Incarcerate*, which traces the rise of mass incarceration and the racial dynamics that accompany it.

The book, which was first published in 1999, won widespread acclaim, and a second edition was printed in 2006. Through a grant program, the publisher, the New Press, was able to send several copies to prisoners around the country.

About a year later, Marc received a package in the mail postmarked from a supermax prison in Connecticut. A recipient of the book had created a graphic novel version of the first chapter. Marc took the illustrations to his editor and struck a deal to create a full-length graphic novel version of *Race to Incarcerate*. But when accessibility to the original artist proved too difficult to maintain, rather than pressing on or scrapping the idea entirely, Marc hired another, established illustrator. This is what we in the movement call *co-opting*.

"We spent quite a bit of time trying to figure out how we could work with Carnell [Hunnicutt] to produce the book, and ultimately, and sadly, it became clear that getting stuff in and out of the prison over and over again just wasn't going to work," Marc said at a recent conference hosted by Stony Brook University. "He was already disfavored by the administration, so with his permission we contracted with an outside illustrator."

Carnell, who spent twenty-nine years inside a high-security prison in Connecticut and was released in 2023, received a one-sentence acknowledgment in the resulting book, *Race to Incarcerate: A Graphic Retelling*. He receives no royalties. And unlike Sabrina Jones, the illustrator who was contracted by the New Press, Carnell has not secured an additional book deal, although now that he is free he is hoping to create a book from his artwork.

"It kind of hurt that he went with someone else," Carnell told me. "I would have done a better job because I was inside looking out. I could have added some things [Jones] couldn't bring to the table."

The profile chapters of this book are bookended by organizations that are run by incarcerated activists Ivan Kilgore and Heshima Denham. This is done intentionally to highlight the importance of placing the most impacted members of oppression at the forefront of this fight. You will hear from them directly, and I encourage you to seek out their independent works. Here, they are speaking through me in hopes that their voices will echo in the halls of power that have denied them visibility.

At the root of all oppressive systems is America's unwillingness to grapple with its history as a nation of colonizers and slaveowners. The prisoners you hear from in this book are enslaved human beings: They work for the state involuntarily for little to no pay. Their experiences are crucial to understanding the uphill battle that lies before us and for attaining a clear picture of the systems we are up against.

A Word about Words

Many of the people you meet in this book will be identified by their first name after the first mention. With the awareness that I am your access point to these individuals, I use this technique to shorten the distance between you and people I've met.

There is one exception, though: I revert to my journalism training when it comes to authors and researchers I have *not* met, simply because I cannot claim to access them with the familiarity I can with the people I've profiled.

Some insufferably long terms lie ahead. While avoiding jargon to the best of my ability, I want to distinguish some words that are intentionally left . . . well . . . wordy, to avoid further dehumanization. If we are to speak to one another with new awareness and compassion, these jargon-curious words and phrases are necessary.

I often use the descriptor *incarcerated individual*, or something like it, to avoid the term *inmate*—a word barked by correctional officers in an attempt to spare themselves the internal torment that spawns from acknowledging the humanity of a person they're tasked with treating like an animal.

All the revolutionary paths discussed in this book have a common theme: They begin and end with the humanity of the systemically oppressed. Removing subjugating nouns from the lexicon is one of many beginnings any personal or communal revolution must include.

Additionally, it will seem, at times, that *racial justice* and *criminal justice* are used interchangeably. I've come to understand the relationship between these terms to be the same as rectangles and squares: All squares are rectangles, but not all rectangles are squares.

Systemic racism exists within a plethora of systems. It saturates economics, education, and politics. The criminal legal system is just one system among several that requires an overhaul. But the racism embedded in our criminal justice system is foundational and, therefore, cannot be removed through a process of incremental reforms. In other words, the system cannot void itself of racism because the system is built upon the intentional subjugation of African Americans. The criminal legal system is the square.

Criminalization, the act of making certain behaviors illegal and punishable by law, was used by post-Emancipation Southern states, still reeling from the economic damage of losing the Civil War, to ensure the continuation of cheap labor and a voting majority. Southern landowners lobbied to criminalize various aspects of Black life in a slew of new laws known as Black Codes. In doing so, whites could convict freedmen of things like felony vagrancy, rent them out to plantation owners in a new system called "convict leasing," and disenfranchise them from the voter rolls because of their criminal history.[4]

The modern criminal justice system likewise provides a significant boost to states' budgets through a sprawling network of factories and surveillance apparatuses, known collectively as the prison-industrial complex. The prison-industrial complex "employs" prisoners for pennies on the dollar to manufacture furniture, sew garments for retail stores, and cultivate agriculture. At the Angola State Prison in Louisiana, as Ken noted, prisoners work the same fields once harvested by slaves and indentured servants. Modern criminalization laws continue the legacy of voter disenfranchisement as well: 4.6 million Americans were barred from voting in 2022 due to a felony conviction.[5]

Similarly, *jails* and *prisons* are linked but not synonymous. Whereas prisons incarcerate individuals convicted of a crime, jails serve several functions within the criminal legal system. Jails primarily contain individuals awaiting trial—those who cannot afford bail, or who are remanded to the state for the risk they allegedly pose to the public—but may also be used for prisoners with short sentences or those who are due to appear in court.

This volume explores several ways antebellum policies have evolved to remain steadfast over centuries. Slavery in America has been fortified with steel bars and brick walls. It has been protected with barbed wire and clever legalese. For this reason, the criminal legal system stands apart from other systems of oppression, but it does not stand alone.

Rethink Your Definition of "Criminal"

Imagine being remembered for your worst day, being tethered to your biggest mistake, with no clear path toward redemption. What we did does not need to define who we are or what we are capable of becoming.

What is "criminal" anyway? The definition varies from era to era, from country to country, and from country to state. Villainous in one jurisdiction may be mundane in another. But imagine if our history books read:

> *Arrestee Gloria Steinem ...*
> *Recidivist Martin Luther King Jr. ...*
> *Federal convict Susan B. Anthony ...*
> *Prisoner 22843 Malcolm X ...*
> *FBI "national threat" Yuri Kochiyama ...*
> *Former lifer Nelson Mandela ...*
> *Ex-con Mohandas Gandhi ...*

Few people are remembered for their interactions with the law. *So why define them this way while they're still alive?* Why is our capacity to see value in an individual nullified by a single moment from their past?

When I talk to people who have been incarcerated—or who are still incarcerated—we rarely discuss their criminal history. Too often, the branding on their state-issued uniforms allows the system to define them. This denies us great humanitarian discoveries. Ask yourself, *At what point do we let go of what someone did, and start to see who they have become?*

If you find yourself wanting to know more about prison life, about the crimes committed by people in prison, and so on, a multitude of books, TV shows, and films are at your disposal. Your curiosity is welcomed, and I will include additional resources where appropriate. This book is a reflection of *my* encounters with the people in the fight for social justice—people I've worked alongside and journalistically observed from afar. My impression of them is rarely influenced by the quarters that confine them or the details of their rap sheet.

This is a book about justice: racial, social, and economic. But it is also an exploration of humanity. How can we decree that killing another person is the most heinous act and then respond by sentencing them to death? When did we espouse the notion that to be free we must cage others? When did "justice" and "vengeance" devolve into synonyms? I hope that this book both changes your views of others' humanity and perhaps provokes an examination of your own.

Anticipation by Gerald Morgan

1

The Way We Move

first met Ali Birts in the spring of 2020. We had just started working together, and between a rare March heat wave, the detailing he was doing on his car, and his daily deliveries of resources to local halfway houses, he was struggling to keep cool. He draped a wet towel around his neck, buzzed his hair, and wore a black t-shirt with a gold fist in the center nearly every day. He took smoke breaks in the shade, standing in front of a fan positioned at the edge of the retractable garage door that served as a window for the office's common area.

But as we rolled into summer, it felt like the world was burning. News about the police shooting an unarmed man—a man who looked like Ali—seemed to be breaking daily. Images of demonstrators, bloodied and blinded from encounters with riot squads, blared across our television sets. We had all been working remotely at that point, connecting virtually for daily all-hands meetings. One morning, a very different Ali popped onto the screen.

"Ali! I like your hair picked out like that, man," said one of my colleagues.

"It's time for a revolution, brotha," Ali replied.

It was a physical manifestation of Ali's radicalization. There was too much work to do for him to focus on his coif; too much rage to channel into a methodical strategy for dismantling the system that leads, according to Ali, to one of two outcomes for people like him: prison or death. All of this collided for Ali in the summer of 2020, and his Afro began to bloom.

Ali spent nearly forty years either in a cell or on the streets. His back often hunches as it loses the fight against years of trudging uphill with a ten-pound sledgehammer and a steel wheelbarrow to mine the rock quarry at Old Folsom prison. He takes marijuana smoke breaks to ease his physical pains. It makes his eyelids heavy, draping over brown irises like protective shields. His voice cracks and his eyes often water when he tells you about his weekend, years of mental anguish flowing through him from extended lockdowns spent inside a stuffy cell, torturing himself over mistakes he made as a kid that would rob him of his young adult years.

Ali was born in Menlo Park, California, and moved to the predominantly white suburbs of nearby Mountain View as a teenager. He was the only Black person at his high school and was constantly abused by racist classmates. He began to cope by fighting back and indulging in drugs. Between the violence and the drug use, he built a substantial conviction history. After decades of cycling in and out of jail, Ali was arrested with a gun in his possession—his "Third Strike" offense. California started counting felony convictions as strikes in the late 1990s, with each new offense allowing judges and prosecutors to inflate the number of years someone had to serve in prison: doubling after the second strike, and extending to twenty-five-to-life after the "strikeout."

Ali languished in state prison until 2000, when a state voter initiative introduced a probationary sentence in lieu of incarceration for people serving life sentences under the Three Strikes law. In the new law's understanding of what is "just" and what is just excessive, Ali deserved thirteen years in prison for the crime he'd been sent there for twenty years ago, so he was released on probation.

As a condition of that probation, Ali had to wear a GPS ankle monitor. He had to pay approximately $840 a month for the monitor, an expense that forced him to live in his car. At sunset, you could find him watching the horizon from a bench in Oakland, tethered to a wall with a spare outlet so the device could recharge. He knew going back to the old neighborhood, where he might be able to crash on someone's couch, would mean going back to his old life, so he made the extremely difficult—and therefore extremely rare—decision to remain unhoused until he could afford a place of his own.

One afternoon, he met up with an old friend, Dorsey Nunn. Dorsey had taken a similar detour through California's cellblocks, but he had been out for several years and was working at an advocacy nonprofit. He took Ali under his wing and walked him through the door of the new civil rights movement.

It turns out, the revolution was closer than Ali may have previously believed. The door he walked through with Dorsey belonged to the headquarters of All of Us or None, an organization advocating for the restoration of civil and human rights for currently and formerly incarcerated people. From chairs arranged in a semicircle, he listened to staff members talk about legislative strategies for a campaign eventually known as Ban the Box, a California statute that removed the "criminal record" indicator from job applications. He heard moving speeches about people "coming home," struggling as he was to adjust to life in the free world while still trapped in the ever-expanding grip of the carceral system.

For the first time since coming home, Ali felt *at* home, felt welcomed and accepted, even with all his cards out on the table. His newfound support system connected him with Project ReMADE, an entrepreneurship training program for formerly incarcerated people run by Stanford Law School. He opened a car detailing business out of his garage and started earning a livable wage. In time, Legal Services for Prisoners with Children, the fiscal sponsor of All of Us or None Oakland, hired him as an organizer.

Ali met me a few years later when I was hired to develop a newspaper for All of Us or None. I was receiving a tutorial on the office's US postage meter as Ali came back from a car rally. He was on fire about the demonstration, relaying to the rest of the staff that participants had stopped traffic in front of the Santa Rita Jail, a facility that has reported sixty-six detainee deaths since 2014. Drivers at the rally held signs, honked their horns, and demanded the release of people inside.

"Blowing the horn and all, that felt good," Ali said. "Whenever I go somewhere it makes me feel good that I'm on the other side of the fence now. No one was out there honking to let Ali out when I was locked up."

I had come to the revolution through the same door as Ali. I remember listening to Dorsey, who had become the executive director of LSPC, give an impassioned speech about this moment in history. He implored the crowd not to think about what they would have done if they had been alive for the 1960s civil rights movement, but rather, "Ask yourselves, 'What am I doing in *this* movement?' What are you doing *right now* to free the oppressed, to make sure our civil rights are restored?"

In rooms like this across the country, people have been sharing their experiences, strategizing ways to shift policies, and preparing for their own moment in history. These are the plotters and planners, the architects of a new movement. This movement looks and feels different from its predecessors, offering new methods of engagement and new paths toward progress.

Modern Abolitionism

Hearing about "abolition" may surface mental images of a stoic Frederick Douglass or an indomitable Harriet Tubman. But members of today's civil rights movement talk about abolition with the same modern currency as they do social media and pop culture.

So why do some people think of abolition as a historical movement and others as a modern one? Simply, some people think slavery is a part of the past, and others think it is part of our present.

Today, more Black people are under correctional control— either in jail or prison, or under supervision by parole or probation departments—than were enslaved in the 1800s.[1] Prison labor, in the manner of its predecessor, convict leasing, generates $11 billion a year in goods and services; workers make, on average, between $0.13 and $0.52 an hour.[2] And despite a cacophony of voices calling for strengthening democracy, 6 million Americans, overwhelmingly non-white citizens, were denied a political voice in the 2020 general election due to disenfranchisement laws and modern-day poll taxes in the form of fluctuating ID requirements, transportation to polling stations placed strategically beyond the bounds of certain neighborhoods, and lack of paid time off to vote.[3] For all these reasons, plus the ongoing violence against Black people, few individuals who examine modern criminal, economic, and political systems believe America has reconciled with its antebellum past. It's a hard argument to deny when a legal exemption for slavery, as noted in the preface, still exists in the country's foundational legal document.

Abolition—the act of abolishing a system, practice, or institution— is a loaded word. We've been ingrained with the belief that our society cannot exist in the absence of certain systems, particularly those concerning law enforcement and punishment. But systems like the American carceral one are unique in their fervor. In 2021 the US incarcerated its citizens at a rate of 664 per 100,000 people. For comparison, in the same year, Russia had a rate of 329 per 100,000, Norway had a rate of 54, and Japan had a rate of 38.[4] The space for exploring alternatives to incarceration is vast, with plenty of examples from developed countries with similar economies and social problems.

For some reason, we just can't shake the need to prescribe subjugation as our sole purveyor of retribution. Locking someone away doesn't bring us comfort: By a margin of three to one, victims of crime prefer holding people accountable through non-carceral options such as mental health treatment, drug treatment, restorative justice, or community service, as revealed in a 2022 survey.[5] Incarceration also doesn't fulfill its promise of rehabilitation or lower crime rates. It is simply what we know, a familiar default we've come to accept as justice.

This stagnancy in our way of thinking about justice and our unwillingness to explore alternative ways of achieving it impact not just America's carceral system but also its political, economic, and social systems. Although each system differs in its impact, all of them marginalize, dehumanize, or deny people from underrepresented communities. However unhappy it makes us, though, we cling to it, willing to make changes here and there but never embracing the bold notion of abolishing it completely.

It seems like everyone took to the streets in the last decade—anti-maskers and neo-Nazis pounded the same pavement (more self-righteously than righteously, of course) as social justice demonstrators and women's rights marchers. Whatever this system is, you have to seriously be reconsidering whether it's working for anyone at this point. But that's for another book. For our purposes, simply remain skeptical—in light of everything you've seen in the last decade especially—that we can continue to try to make the old way work. The barrier for entry into this book is abolitionist thought, because I have come to understand that no change to the current system can eradicate the inherent racism embedded in its foundation. Our society functions, by design, by working the many and benefitting the few. Going forward, let's challenge the idea that racial equality can be attained through reforming a system that has, for the last 400 years, oppressed non-white individuals under its control.

An estimated 26 million people in the United States participated in demonstrations against police brutality in June 2020 alone, the largest showing of resistance in the history of the country.[6] The following year, police killed more people than in any other year in a decade, only to outdo themselves again in 2022.[7] *This movement must be different from the ones before it.*

Your dedicated trudging was not all for naught, nor is your feverish desire to hit the streets misguided. Showings of large-scale crowds protesting an injustice still signal to those vying for political power what they should consider in their platforms—and to those who are suffering under those injustices that they are not alone. This demonstration of solidarity is certainly meaningful, but this book will ask you to take additional steps, off the main drag. The strategies included here require an exercise not only in walking new paths but in finding new ways of thinking. For starters, consider this simple question:

At a point in history when we are being forced to reimagine everything from remote work to energy resources, why not take the whole thing back to the drawing board?

A Whole New World

When Disney+ came out in November 2019, my son was almost two years old, and my husband and I were eager to introduce him to the classics. We started with *The Lion King*, which prompted the following suggestions: *The Lion King* (live-action), *The Lion King II: Simba's Pride*, *The Lion King 1½*, *Around the World with Timon & Pumbaa*, and two television series (*The Lion Guard* and *The Lion King's Timon & Pumbaa*). We discovered there were endless sequels, prequels, and spin-offs of the movies we'd grown up with, as well as fourteen live-action remakes and a dozen more in the works.

I'm not sure which came first—the realization that studios could make money by dusting off old ideas, or the slowdown of generating new ones—and I'm not sure it matters. What does matter is how this creative void stalls our efforts to move forward when it counts.

During the pandemic, I remember seeing a photograph of a poker table in Las Vegas cut up with plexiglass dividers. Unable to come up with an alternative structure to address safety during a time of many unknowns, Vegas simply rebooted the old system with some minor tweaks. The result? In the five weeks after Las Vegas reopened, the number of daily COVID-19 cases rose tenfold.[8]

Meanwhile, one group decided to try an entirely new approach. Scientists, opting to inject messenger cells into the body rather than a dumbed-down version of the virus itself, trimmed decades off the process of bringing a new vaccine to market. The time it took Pfizer and Moderna to manufacture a first-of-its-kind vaccine and earn FDA approval was objectively a scientific feat. *Could a similar diversion from the traditional way of doing things work for, say, civil rights work? Could an alternate path lead to an expedited arrival of a more equitable society?*

Let's first consider whether the current system can be "fixed." Surely the solution would be drawn from the same source as the solution to most other modern-day problems: technology. However, our attempt to apply technology to the criminal justice system, in particular, has faltered at every turn, sometimes causing even more harm to Black and Latino communities. Centuries of over-policing inner cities, racial profiling, and policies like stop-and-frisk have generated a statistically biased—read: racist—control group. Consequently, any datasets governing technology for use in the criminal justice system are unreliable. The current system's innovations, like pretrial risk assessment tools—algorithm-based software that purportedly predicts an arrestee's risk of committing a new crime, being rearrested, or failing to appear in court—are not only dubious but, more likely, dangerous to vast swaths of marginalized communities.

I was a skeptical reporter when pretrial risk assessment tools were becoming popular about a decade ago, wary of previous evolutions that had only led to an expansion of prison. The advent of GPS monitors, as Ali's experience exemplified, extended the reach and control of the prison system the wearer had supposedly been freed from. The promise of technology as a fix to almost anything, however, was making pretrial risk assessment tools the preferred method of determining pretrial detainment over cash bail by reformists. Chesa Boudin, who challenged the constitutionality of cash bail as San Francisco's deputy public defender, was one such reformist. I called him for an article I was writing about what a post-bail system might look like.

A Rhodes scholar with a JD from Yale, Chesa was eloquent and convincing in explaining his crusade to end cash bail, although he didn't have to be. The idea that you can be detained for long periods when you're innocent and poor, but free to roam about when you're guilty and rich, makes for a pretty strong argument against the practice. Chesa didn't offer any thoughts on the use of pretrial risk assessment tools, but he gave fiery answers on monetary bail and launched into a broader conversation about the disadvantages poor people and communities of color face when they come up against the criminal legal system.

It was political rhetoric at its best—his seamless diversion from the algorithmic solution that, my investigation ultimately found, had designated 73 percent of pretrial defendants in Los Angeles as high risk, a number that should have been closer to 10 percent—and I shouldn't have been surprised when Chesa ran for district attorney of San Francisco.[9] To some it may have seemed odd, a man who'd served as a public defender now aiming for the top spot on the opposite side of the justice system, but Chesa's campaign came on the heels of several similar ones. Larry Krasner, elected to run the Philadelphia DA's office in 2017, was also a criminal defense attorney. Kim Foxx, who was elected Illinois state's attorney in Cook County—which includes Chicago and is the second-largest prosecutorial office in the country—in 2016, ran on a platform of police accountability and overturning wrongful convictions. In fact, by the time Chesa announced his bid for DA in 2019, seven other prosecutors had already run and won on reform-based platforms.[10]

Chesa's story and campaign were compelling. Both of his parents were sent to prison when he was a toddler, and he spoke passionately about the broader ecosystem of people harmed by crime—loved ones left with broken families, and communities devastated by the economic toll of endless criminalization. Between his moving speeches about his personal experiences and his keen intellect, he was a reporter's dream. Often when I'd write articles about his campaign, this wonderful phenomenon in journalism would occur: An elegant and enticing opening paragraph formed almost effortlessly, the perfect sequence of words bubbling up from pages of notes. As we say in the biz, the lede—the opening line or paragraph of an article—wrote itself.

This intrigue also worked on the voting populace, with Chesa ultimately defeating a more moderate candidate, Suzy Loftus, who had been serving as the interim district attorney. I sent him a congratulatory message, then my resumé, and by Christmas I was heading up to San Francisco from LA to serve as his communications manager.

The movement of observers of the criminal legal system into advocacy jobs—such as my journey from criminal justice reporter to DA speechwriter—is not uncommon. In 2020 former Buzzfeed News legal editor Chris Geidner became the strategy director of the Justice Collaborative, a sort of consulting company for criminal justice nonprofits and progressive political candidates. CNN host Van Jones cofounded the nonprofit Dream Corps, an incubator for bipartisan criminal justice reform work. A year into his volunteer work inside prison, producer Scott Budnick abruptly left the film industry in 2013, using his profits from *The Hangover* movies to launch the nonprofit Anti-Recidivism Coalition. He returned to the silver screen in 2019 to produce *Just Mercy*, a very unfunny biopic about civil rights attorney Bryan Stevenson. A need to immediately become more involved in addressing the problem of mass incarceration has been a natural response of those who simply look the system in the face.

A disclaimer: This relationship between Chesa and me does not end well. The day before the U-Haul arrived to pick up the last of the boxes in Los Angeles, Chesa sent me a late-night text saying we needed to discuss an exit strategy—*my* exit strategy—because of "messaging issues." I still don't fully understand his reasons. My messaging had seemed on point during his inaugural speech, which I drafted, but perhaps I was naive to believe those social justice–infused talking points would continue once he took office. We ultimately agreed to change my role to a "transitional" position, one designed to bridge the gap between his campaign comms team and the office comms team.

In all honesty, there is no lingering bitterness when it comes to my time with the DA. Fairly soon after I started, it became obvious that the idea of reforming the criminal justice system from within was a fantasy. You may think of so-called progressive prosecutors as the Vegas plexiglass of the criminal legal system. They run on promises to fix the problem from the inside out, and then do just enough to stem the bleeding without ever treating the hemorrhage. Their job, ultimately, is to prosecute, to send people into a confined setting that offers little in the form of rehabilitation or paths to redemption.

On the third day of Chesa's tenure, he held an all-hands meeting in the office's main conference room. I stood in the back, examining the body language of an edgy collection of suited attorneys. Lawyers tend to like clean lines, and the idea of having someone they used to go up against in court now calling the shots was less than ideal.

Some among the old guard had a different attitude, though. When Chesa approached the podium to make his address, their faces began to betray coy smiles. They looked at the thirty-nine-year-old attorney the way I look at my toddler son when he tries to eat Cheerios with a spoon and manages to get only one in his mouth. He was young compared to most of the staff, and his lanky body defeated any attempt to be intimidating, but the comparison here is more akin to the almost-adorable misconceived determination that Chesa shared with my cereal-fumbling child.

These deputies had already been through the tenure of progressive prosecutor George Gascón, Chesa's predecessor. In his eight-year stint as DA, Gascón, who promised police accountability in his campaign, was never able to charge a fatal-force case against a police officer, including the highly publicized 2015 shooting of Mario Woods. This void in Gascón's term, I would soon learn from my coworkers, tormented him. His administrative assistants said he would look physically ill during the months of protests when grieving families would occupy the steps of the courthouse, pleading for justice. The reality is that progressive prosecutors, hamstrung by legal protections for officers and staff resistant to change, make little headway when it comes to progress. Between 2013 and 2020, a timeframe that perfectly lines up with the rise in progressive prosecutors, only 142 of the 8,710 deaths caused by police led to criminal charges against the responsible officer or officers. Thirteen of those homicides led to the officer serving time in prison—*13 out of over 8,000*.[11] That means less than 2 percent of police who kill are charged and less than 1 percent are imprisoned for their actions. This rate has held steady, as officers kill over 1,000 people each year.

At best, DAs like Chesa realize too late that the system is far more complex than they had believed, and their staff far less cooperative than they'd hoped. At worst, they are politicians knowing what they need to say to win an election.

Chesa was recalled by voters in 2021, unable to balance the implementation of progressive measures and a narrative that made the community feel safe. Ultimately, he was trying to slow a freight train powered partly by the old guard members of his own office. His strategy was always doomed, and it doesn't matter whether he knew or not.

"Because It's a Revolution!"

So now what? Where do we go from here? We find ourselves in the eye of a perfect storm. Civil unrest blares across our television sets in response to police violence, health care is in crisis, and environmental degradation is forcing us to reimagine every aspect of our lives. It is not enough to learn how we got here. We must start to imagine where we go *from* here.

The following pages detail the strategies of four modern abolitionist organizations. While movements require forceful interventions on multiple fronts, one particular focus is highlighted for each chapter to exemplify how an individual oppressive system can be targeted. I encourage you to look more deeply at any or all of these organizations, should their mission speak to you, and research the array of opportunities they offer for engagement.

The architects of change you meet here are reimagining communities, punishment, economics, and infrastructure. To understand these systems, we'll first examine them individually, uncovering how they were conceived, how they operate, and the reasons they have failed the majority of residents in this country. With these discoveries in mind, we'll examine the blueprints of organizations looking to dismantle current systems and rebuild more equitable ones. Some of these strategies redefine systems completely, while others borrow from existing systems to create new futures.

At the heart of each chapter is each visionary's humanity. These are access points for you to see and understand their fight for liberation, in addition to their qualifications. They are driven and connected by their *identity politics*, a contemporary term for describing the coalescence of individuals of a specific marginalized constituency based on their shared desire for political freedom. This bond, strengthened like a diamond under pressure and constraint, has proven more infallible than those centered around belief systems, manifestos, or party affiliations. As such, they promise to triumph over and outlast outdated beliefs, corrupt rhetoric, and wavering political parties.

As this book's title suggests, we're going to be discussing revolution. It's a word that's popping up more and more with very little context and even less understanding. At the US Capitol riot on January 6, 2021, for example, a camera crew ran up on a woman sobbing and holding her face. "They maced me," she said, shocked at the apparently new idea that actions have consequences. The reporter asked what she was doing when this happened, and she said she was attempting to (unlawfully) break into the Capitol building. When asked why she tried to break in, she responded, "Because it's a revolution!"[12]

Girl.

Revolution, a political science term, is a fight for a fundamental change in political power that's forced by the general masses organizing and overtaking an oppressive regime. The January 6 rioters were not fighting on behalf of the masses. They were fighting against the masses, attempting to overturn the results of a flawed but democratic election. Neither were they fighting to even the playing field, as exhibited by the "Camp Auschwitz" t-shirts and the Confederate flags being paraded through the Capitol. These are the vestiges of a political system that requires a revolution, not the values that power revolution.

"Elizabeth from Tennessee," as the indignant rioter came to be named, was right about one thing: Revolution is necessary. As Michelle Alexander writes in her seminal book *The New Jim Crow*, "A civil war had to be waged to end slavery; a mass movement was necessary to bring a formal end to Jim Crow. Those who imagine that far less is required to dismantle mass incarceration and build a new, egalitarian racial consensus reflecting a compassionate rather than punitive impulse toward poor people of color fail to appreciate the distance between Martin Luther King Jr.'s dream and the ongoing racial nightmare for those locked up and locked out of American society."[13]

This book details strategies on how to move toward a reimagined society. These movements are powered by people whose personal experiences have informed their paths. You are welcome to join them or find your own track. Just don't turn away, because, like it or not, the revolution is here.

Race to Incarcerate: Introduction to Conclusion P. 1 by Carnell Hunnicutt Sr.

2

Systems of Oppression

Yes: make them aware of the possibilities they have denied themselves or the passiveness they have displayed in situations where it was really necessary to cling to the heart of the world, like a splinter—to force, if needed, the rhythm of the world's heart; dislocate, if needed, the system of controls; but in any case, most certainly, face the world.

—FRANTZ FANON, *Black Skin, White Masks*

Before we get into the stories and strategies of people fighting oppressive systems, let's get clear about what they're up against.

The four systems examined in this volume—community development, punishment, economics, and infrastructure—are all essential elements of society, but the way they are applied in the United States skews heavily to benefit only a few members of that society. This is not solely because of racial harassment or discrimination. A system that deploys ad hoc violence or discrimination may contribute to the historical trauma of any one group, but it could also be overthrown by counter-violence. The result would still be a lack of equality, but power would shift from one group to another. What makes racial justice and social justice in the US unique is that our systems do not operate this way. Institutionalized racism created certain "norms" or "realities" that led to a single, perpetual benefactor to the power structure in this country: wealthy, white men.

The most glaring and consequential example of this is America's "War on Drugs." The impetus for modern criminalization stems from policies instituted by Richard Nixon in the 1970s and reinforced by Ronald Reagan in the 1980s. An influx of funds to drug enforcement agencies and policies aimed at criminalizing drug use led to a rapid increase in incarceration rates and disproportionate sentencing of Black and white defendants.

The "reality" presented to the public was the government being "tough on crime," but behind closed doors, another motive was revealed. During a 1994 interview, President Nixon's domestic policy chief, John Ehrlichman, was quoted as saying: "We knew we couldn't make it illegal to be either against the war or Black, but by getting the public to associate the hippies with marijuana and Blacks with heroin, and then criminalizing both heavily, we could disrupt those communities. We could arrest their leaders, raid their homes, break up their meetings, and vilify them night after night on the evening news. Did we know we were lying about the drugs? Of course, we did."[1] Thus, under the guise of "tough on crime," a racially motivated policy earns widespread acceptance.

This book will examine many conflicts between "Black" and "white," but it's important to keep in mind that before there was such a distinction, the only differentiator between members of society was power. As colonizers, white settlers quickly established themselves atop the societal hierarchy by forcefully occupying the country. The colonizers' weapons were more deadly and they hailed from a society defined by class—a wealth-based system designed to keep the rich rich and the poor poor. It was a system entirely foreign to the

Indigenous people who were killed and displaced en masse for the sake of land and power grabs.

The social construct of "race" in America grew out of this need to hoard wealth. Most historians point to Bacon's Rebellion, a 1676 revolt of white and Black indentured servants and slaves, as the establishing point for racial hierarchy in the country. It began as a feud between colonial governor William Berkeley and Virginian settler Nathaniel Bacon when Berkeley refused Bacon's request to drive the Native Americans out of Virginia. In retaliation, Bacon organized a militia of underclass whites and Black slaves. Together, the band of rebels brought the town of Jamestown to its knees; the militia overtook plantations and burnt them to the ground. Their success inspired similar bands of Blacks and poor whites, united by a common oppressor in the wealthy landowner. So landowners and politicians designed laws to criminalize Black life and formed slave patrols, groups of lower-caste whites who were given the authority to enforce those new laws. Where unity between poor whites and Black slaves had been found by calling to attention their mutual oppression by wealthy landowners, legal language now called attention to their most obvious difference: the technically free and the determinedly captured.

"[The white working-class's] contradictory behavior is explained by feelings of loyalty to race, by their identification with the white hierarchy, and by their economic advantage over the oppressed races," George Jackson wrote from his prison cell, later published in the book *Blood in My Eye*. "They may be oppressed themselves, but in return, they are allowed to oppress millions of others."[2]

Race as a social construct can be seen quite clearly in the constant recategorization of "non-whites." The "new" immigrants who began arriving from Poland, Greece, Ireland, and Italy at the beginning of the twentieth century were put in a sort of racial limbo, told by the ruling class that they were not considered white, nor were they considered Black, but rather somewhere in between. Caricatured in propaganda, Irishmen were apes, Jews had mythical witch-like noses, and Chinese immigrants were drawn as parasitical locusts.[3] New immigrants still posed a threat as "others," but they had come here willingly—versus Africans ripped from their homeland and sold off as commodities upon arrival—from primarily European countries. The difference allowed them a chance for mobility. As Henry Pratt Fairchild, an influential American sociologist, wrote in 1911, "If [the white immigrant] proves himself a man, and . . . acquires wealth and cleans himself up—very well, we might receive him in a generation or two. But at present he is far beneath us, and the burden of proof rests with him."[4] This further served to define "whiteness" as the norm, a preferred classification to "Blackness."

The fallout of Bacon's Rebellion—fear-stoked policies that generated a caste apparatus based on race rather than wealth—created opportunity for multigenerational oppressive systems. These systems have served to maintain a social hierarchy where both economics and race hold proximity to power. In the historical context of how "whiteness" was constructed, it is interesting that race, not power, is something that can be "earned," as indicated by Fairchild.

The purpose of grassroots movements, particularly the ones examined in this volume, is to disrupt this hierarchy by redefining the systems that uphold it. This is not a practice of dismantlement. Rather, it is a practice of building up the essential elements of society toward more equitable ends.

"What is, so to speak, the object of abolition?" scholars Fred Moten and Stefano Harney write in their critical analysis of public policy through a Black radical lens. "Not so much the abolition of prisons but the abolition of a society that would have prisons, that could have slavery, that could have the wage, and therefore not abolition as the elimination of anything but abolition as the founding of a new society."[5]

Community Development

An excellent microcosm of the impact of oppressive systems is community development, simply because the driving forces of such systems are felt most acutely in society's individual fragments.

Often, the boundaries that define a community are a result of policies aimed at social control. As freed slaves moved out of the American South in the nineteenth and twentieth centuries, the federal government intervened to define communities by race. When the country entered World War II, the government provided housing for the influx of workers who had moved to cities like Richmond, California, where military production was ramping up. These accommodations were segregated; Black workers were designated to makeshift, temporary housing, with their white counterparts situated near white residential suburbs in more sturdily constructed homes.[6] In St. Louis, zoning laws prohibited pollution-generating industries, liquor stores, and prostitution houses in white neighborhoods but not Black neighborhoods. Residents of neighborhoods with such industry were then precluded from the Federal Housing Authority's insured amortized mortgages. The price of homeownership went up, and the ability to make repairs went down, leaving many homes dilapidated.[7]

As the country developed into a sprawling landscape of suburbs, farms, and cities, government agencies—from local city planners to state legislatures and federal institutions—solidified their role in keeping Black and white neighborhoods separate and distinct. In chapter 3, when Ivan says he lived on the "other side of the tracks" from his white classmates, he is speaking literally: Federal- and state-sanctioned development of railroads and highways has been intentionally designed to separate neighborhoods defined by race and class.

"Without our government's purposeful imposition of racial segregation," writes Richard Rothstein in The Color of Law (a must-read for anyone interested in the subject of "de jure" segregation), "the other causes—private prejudice, white flight, real estate steering, bank redlining, income differences, and self-segregation—still would have existed but with far less opportunity for expression."[8]

In a sense, the purpose of community zoning in the current system would be containment. Zoning is a way of taking necessary elements of society—industry, diversity, housing, and the like—and placing those considered unattractive to white homeowners in a neighborhood of "others." As a result, neighborhoods with large minority populations are often near toxic factories and far from quality grocers, creating "food deserts."

This separation is felt deeply, both consciously and unconsciously, by community members. All the aforementioned examples force a feeling of otherness on people who have been lumped in with society's "necessary evils," and their subsequent criminalization solidifies the message that their place has been assigned. As carceral geographer Ruth Wilson Gilmore says in her seminal book *Golden Gulag*, "California's indeterminate sentences extended to life sentences for Black, Latino, and white prisoners whose failure to be rehabilitated translated as their refusal to learn their proper places in the social order."[9]

Systems of "order" in communities rarely derive from the community itself. Occupational reporting data collected by the US Census Bureau in 2020, for example, found that the share of white police officers was larger than the share of white residents in 99 of the country's 100 largest metropolitan areas. In several of those areas, police were whiter than their assigned communities by 20 percentage points.[10] Political representation is also seemingly "outside the bounds"— roughly 62 million eligible voters live in districts considered shoo-ins for the political party they oppose.[11] In short, communities are rarely governed, secured, or resourced by the people who live within their bounds.

Punishment

To understand prison abolition, it's worth tracking the changing purpose of prison from a rehabilitative vehicle informed by religious practices to punishment and isolation.

First implemented in the US in the eighteenth century, prisons were a religious reform to the death penalty, forcing someone to be alone with their Maker and repent for their sins. Jonas Hanway, one of the most prominent representatives of this line of thought, proliferated this theory: "The repentance and amendment, the sorrow for the past, and the resolution with regard to the future part of life, will be more sincere in the prison than it usually is in the church."[12]

At their inception, prisons were also meant as a deterrent for crime, entering American society on the heels of theories like John Locke's "sensation psychology," which suggested that conduct was the product of one's social environment.[13] Prison as a deterrent has never been proven in practice partly because, contrary to Locke's philosophy, it imposes social environments that are harsh and violent.

Prison's evolution into the prison-industrial complex has been spurred on by the movement from religious reformation to a political need for control and sustained power.

"Crime means violation of the law," Gilmore writes. "Laws change, depending on what, in a social order, counts as stability, and who, in a social order, needs to be controlled."[14]

The relationship between control and incarceration is far more intertwined than crime and incarceration. During Reconstruction, politicians in the North and South criminalized Black life through a series of laws known as Black Codes. The aforementioned motive for Nixon's War on Drugs offers a modern-day example, though presented less overtly than policies in the antebellum South.

What has been made plain to the public is that rehabilitation is no longer the primary concern of correctional facilities. Even in so-called progressive states like California, legislative language heightens the need for "punishment" over rehabilitation when it comes to imprisonment.[15] As Supreme Court Justice Clarence Thomas wrote in a 2023 ruling, "Congress has chosen finality over error correction."[16]

"Incapacitation doesn't pretend to change anything about people except where they are," Gilmore surmises. "It is in a simple-minded way, then, a geographical solution that purports to solve social problems by extensively and repeatedly removing people from disordered, deindustrialized milieus and depositing them somewhere else."[17]

The state also has a financial motive to keep prisoners. In 2019 three men in California's prison fire brigade died fighting wildfires that devastated entire towns within the state. They made about $3 per day, plus an additional buck during active emergencies. They worked alongside firefighters earning an average of $91,000 a year, before overtime and bonuses.[18] In fact, California has become so dependent on its over 1,000 incarcerated firefighters that, when emergency decarceration efforts began during the COVID pandemic, a corrections officer was quoted as saying, "How do you justify releasing all these inmates in prime fire season with all these fires going on?"[19]

On a national scale, 3M, Western Union, Amazon, and Microsoft have all relied on the labor of incarcerated people. These are 4 of over 4,100 companies that profit from prison labor.[20] During the height of the pandemic, people in prisons all over the country working for little to no money made hand sanitizer and face masks to help fight COVID-19, as they struggled to access these protective measures themselves.

These financial "benefits" contribute to the power aspect of the prison-industrial complex (PIC)—but more profound is how the PIC exerts control. In 2023 the United States had 1,566 state prisons, 98 federal prisons, 1,323 juvenile correctional facilities, 3,116 local jails, 181 immigration detention facilities, and 80 Indian country jails. This isn't counting the military prisons, or prisons in US territories.[21] Incapacitation of whole communities certainly speaks for itself, but beyond concrete facilities, the PIC has broadened into an intricate web of government, business, and law enforcement entities that use surveillance and policing, in addition to imprisonment, as solutions to economic, social, and political disorder. It includes electronic monitoring devices, CCTV cameras, and cell phone tracking devices, all accessible to law enforcement with little oversight.[22]

Prisons have moved far from the rehabilitation facilities originally pitched by religious sociologists. They have "industrialized" both a labor force and an advanced surveillance market and created a "complex" web of influence that allows prison officials to operate far beyond prison walls.

Economy

In 2021 the *Harvard Gazette* estimated that the net wealth of a typical American Black family was around one-tenth that of a white family.[23]

This discrepancy, and several other economic disparities in America, has come to be known as the *racial wealth gap*—an inequality entrenched in the American banking system, and a natural byproduct of American capitalism.

It is widely held by economists that capitalism traces back to Adam Smith, an eighteenth-century Scottish philosopher who detailed the system's main principles in his book *An Inquiry into the Nature and Causes of the Wealth of Nations*. According to Smith, the driving forces behind the economy were the division of labor and self-interest.[24] Essentially, *The Wealth of Nations* proclaimed that economic progress was dependent on working-class members of society, who were driven to produce by their natural desire to generate individual wealth. This, in turn, would lead to financial gain in all of society, with money circulating through the population like blood through a body.

The book was published in 1776, a time when political, religious, and scientific revolutions were taking place across the globe. Having just freed themselves from the British, American colonists were quick to engage with a newly defined economic system that had been examined in a scientific matter. And similar to Americans at that time, Smith was willing to overlook some of self-interest's more problematic developments, such as slavery. *The Wealth of Nations*, published at the height of the transatlantic slave trade, makes no mention of slavery in its nearly 800 pages of examination. Instead, self-interest—specifically that of white male landowners—dominates both the book and the motivations of capitalist designers, the idea of profits over all else.

Smith intended to evolve economic philosophy from a zero-sum game—where profits to one must mean losses to another—into one of infinite potential for progress. So why does it seem like American capitalism is a constant rat race with very few beneficiaries? Fanon puts it succinctly: "Society, unlike biochemical processes, does not escape human influence."[25]

A few specific perversions of Smith's work have manifested over the years. Ayn Rand's *The Fountainhead* transformed self-interest from a psychological issue to a moral one, professing that those who were not driven to improve their own circumstances were lesser beings. We can hear this echo in the 1980s' "crack whore" and "welfare queen" rhetoric that proliferated during the War on Drugs. Morality and wealth become so intertwined that successful people are considered right while others are considered at best broken, at worst criminal.

The second issue is that Smith's principles of division of labor and self-interest are elevated over the human cost to achieve these things. For example, an immigrant farm worker might live in barrack-like housing while harvesting crops, the sales of which primarily benefit the landowners and families who have acquired large-acreage farms. Both worker and landowner are technically motivated by self-interest, but the latter's interest is in accumulation while the former's interest is survival—an average farmworker made $14.62 per hour in 2020, half the hourly wage for all workers that year.[26]

These distortions of Smith's theory contribute to capitalism's exacerbation of inequality. The separation of economic logic from social and human experience is what allowed the Portuguese to erect "barracoons" along the coast of Africa in the eighteenth century. These barracoons, a word meaning "factories," produced people as commodities: Africans who were shipped as cargo in the transatlantic slave trade. As the slave trade grew, the Dutch, French, and British also established so-called factories through which human cargoes were ushered onto ships.

The American banking system, working with little oversight in the name of—wait for it—self-interest, has instituted an unequal distribution of the kind of capital that allows upward mobility to begin. (Let's not forget that even the conquistadors needed financial backing from private-sector financiers.) The government has done this through insured amortized mortgages, as well as municipal zoning laws, while banks have dealt a final blow to minority families in more overtly racist ways.

In 2011 the US Justice Department determined that loan officers from Bank of America subsidiary Countrywide Financial charged higher fees and rates to more than 200,000 minority borrowers than to white borrowers who posed the same credit risk. Ten thousand of those minority borrowers were steered by the bank into costly sub-prime mortgages; white borrowers with similar credit profiles received regular loans.[27]

Countrywide's actions don't take the government off the hook for this discrepancy. The lax-regulation laws enacted in the name of self-interest created this lack of oversight. It also reveals why relief from government entities seems far-fetched.

"We cannot understand the income and wealth gap that persists between African Americans and whites without examining governmental policies that purposely kept black incomes low throughout most of the twentieth century," Rothstein writes. "Once government implemented these policies, economic differences became self-perpetuating."[28]

Examples include the government protecting the bargaining rights of unions that denied African Americans membership, or segregated them into low-income jobs, a federal protection that began with the New Deal and lasted until the 1960s.[29] Government-sanctioned denial of VA and GI loans in the 1930s has left generations of Black Americans playing catch-up to try to establish firm financial footing from which they may grasp Smith's "infinite potential."

Infrastructure

Interstate 10 in Southern California, also known as the Santa Monica Freeway, is always jammed. Combined with the intersecting 405, the smog emanating from trucks and commuters is what gives Los Angeles its orange hue as the sun sets. It is a bane to most people who live there and, more acutely, to those who no longer live there.

The fourteen-lane expanse was designed in the 1930s as Los Angeles's first freeway. At that time, an affluent Black suburb known as Sugar Hill lay directly in the proposed path. Residents protested, but construction pressed on, cutting through Sugar Hill, demolishing homes, and displacing residents. This strategy continued as the federal government enacted its interstate highway program some two decades later. The 1950s interstate highway development boom permanently displaced roughly 100,000 families, mostly housed in minority-majority neighborhoods, without providing comparable or affordable alternatives.[30] In doing so, the government systematically cut down every opportunity for African American communities to advance within the existing structure. Those who did find upward economic traction were quickly confronted with new barriers, some with six lanes of traffic.

Infrastructure, seen through the lens of systemic oppression, encompasses more than roads and highways. If society were a grand banquet, infrastructure would be the necessary attributes to accommodate such a gathering: Beyond the road that leads guests to it, the party needs a home, financing, security, and food on the table. All these things are created by interconnected mechanisms that create what we will term here as *infrastructure.*

The essential element of infrastructure that leaves it vulnerable to manipulation is accessibility. While working-class farmers, construction workers, tellers, and laborers tirelessly power the engine that drives infrastructure, a powerful few other people hold the keys and steer the machine. They turn it on and off at will, decide the direction of travel, and are the sole beneficiaries of whatever profits are reaped in the process.

Nonfiguratively, this dynamic is exemplified in banking institutions that deny opportunities for homeownership, or upward mobility, through practices dictated by executives. In agriculture, this can translate to farmers hiring low-income workers to tow the fields while distributing the produce in grocery stores outside the food-desert neighborhoods where those workers live.

Racism embedded in infrastructure becomes self-perpetuating. Infrastructure is easily normalized because it is essential to any society. When covertly injected with racism, however, infrastructure can develop horizontal prejudice, a phenomenon in which a group oppressed by a system ends up furthering that system. For example, Gilmore examines the tendency of communities in crisis to seek aid in the very systems forcing those crises upon them. In her research into the 500 percent increase in the California prison population between 1982 and 2000, Gilmore details the state's prison construction project, the largest in the world according to a number of analysts. The corrections department, which had ballooned to nearly 10 percent of California's operating budget and worked with little oversight, targeted rural towns in the state's Central Valley, where workforces had been devastated by mechanization, drought, and a monopolized growing system that had benefited only the four families who operated the farms at the time. As a result, Central Valley counties consistently ranked among the wealthiest agricultural counties in the United States, but among the state's poorest per capita income.[31]

Residents were quick to jump on the promise the corrections department made to inject capital into the town by means of prison development. New jobs would be created for construction as well as employment once the prison was up and running. By counting prisoners among the county's "residents," towns could claim greater subsidies from the legislature without actually having to invest in the surplus population.

Little to none of this manifested in rural California. The increased residency served only the local politicians, who now represented densely populated districts beholden to a few actual constituents. The prison jobs went to veteran correctional officers who transferred from other facilities and took up residence outside the town's boundaries. With the facilities housing the state's "dangerous" population looming in the background, retail and entertainment stayed far beyond the towns that had hoped to glean some economic benefit. And while the prisons did spend large amounts of money on the facilities they built, these profits were poured into nonlocal infrastructural controllers, such as electricity, gas, and water utilities.

As Gilmore writes, "There was no discussion about what it meant for a small city dominated by a single-industry oligopoly to deal with inequality by bringing in an enormous new employer outside the direct control of anybody."[32]

The farms that combined under single families, exploited cheap labor, and lined the pockets of just a handful of people: that's infrastructure. Prison construction: that's infrastructure. Utilities: that's infrastructure. Each element that defines the potential and realities of communities is carefully conscripted to maintain the status quo. Residents reach out for a solution to the only system they see as capable of providing resources. It is the very system that offered empty promises to begin with, but what is the alternative? They wash, rinse, and repeat until so entangled they deny themselves any hope of escape.

Invisible Boundaries

This book mentions justice a lot: criminal justice, social justice, racial justice . . . At last count, the word *justice* appears 120 times. So what is it?

In general, we're examining justice as the antidote to the aforementioned systems of oppression. But specifically, the definition varies greatly from person to person. It may seem trivial, but take a moment to generate your own definition of justice. When engaging in such a fight, it is essential to know what you're fighting for.

Systems of oppression have commonalities. Each system produces racial disparities, although the mechanisms or policies themselves may not seem overtly racist. They include both visible and invisible boundaries that limit access and deny mobility, either physical, social, or financial. Where these boundaries intersect may hold the key to fighting these systems on multiple fronts, finding ways to reconfigure them or remove them entirely.

I remember seeing a video of an art installation featuring traffic cones on a New York City sidewalk. In an attempt to expose society's herd mentality, the artist placed four or five traffic cones in a circle, then a square, then forming two lanes. With each iteration, pedestrians maneuvered accordingly, walking along the arch for the circle, quickly sidestepping around the square, and creating single-file lines through the lanes. There was nothing to avoid, no harm or obstruction along the path. Just an invisible boundary that people followed without questioning.

Some boundaries are meant to keep us safe, but others are imagined. The key to unveiling systems of oppression is asking questions about what line has been drawn. If it is not keeping you safe, just move the cones.

Not Feeling the Freedom by Scotty Scott aka Scott W. Smith

Reimagining Communities:
Ivan Kilgore, United Black Family Scholarship Foundation

van Kilgore and I connect late at night, after my kid goes to bed and before California State Prison, Solano, begins to lock down. We talk over video conference, me in front of my computer, the retina display cutting through the darkness of my sleepy house, and Ivan on a choppy tablet, the dayroom's fluorescent lights beaming down on him. He's usually wearing a skullcap and a white t-shirt that make him stand out from the backdrop of iron bars and concrete walls. His skin is a light shade of brown, a hue he inherited from scattered interracial marriages among his family tree: His mother was born to a Black woman and an Irishman, and his father's father was the son of a predatorial slaveowner. A close-trimmed beard outlines Ivan's billowing cheeks and sharp jawline. He has a stocky build, with broad shoulders, a figure that would have cast a large shadow over the young man who entered the California prison system two decades ago.

Ivan has spent the last three of his twenty-four years in prison in his six-by-eight-foot cell at Solano. An avid reader, he's amassed an array of books from the prison library. They line the plastic shelving opposite his bed, with condiments and toiletries serving as bookends. A stack of research papers shares the middle shelf with commissary goods like salt, hot sauce, a bowl, and a coffee mug. Under that are two levels of neatly stacked documents, containing everything from court filings to foundation records and personal writings. Since Ivan doesn't currently have to share a cell, these compositions overflow onto the empty top bunk in tidy, organized piles.

A small table with a round-top stool drilled into the back wall serves as the epicenter of Ivan's operations. On a heavy, clear-case typewriter, he coauthors research papers, writes scholarly articles for university projects, files lawsuits, motions, and petitions on behalf of himself and other prisoners, and drafts manuscripts for his future publications. It's also where he conducts meetings for the United Black Family Scholarship Foundation, a nonprofit he established from prison in 2014 to architect a unique, multifaceted movement for Black liberation. With only two available electrical outlets, the typewriter is on rotation with a thirteen-inch television, a radio, and his prison-issued tablet. The wires for these devices crisscross along the concrete, creating frames around a mirror, a poster of an Islamic prayer, and a picture of Malcolm X.

Solano is the fourth prison where Ivan has been incarcerated. He transferred there from Salinas Valley and, before that, spent time at San Quentin and New Folsom. Each prison's program offerings and work detail has varied from the others, but Ivan has felt a distinct continuity in how the prison system treats the population it controls. Ivan believes in abolition not because it would mean his freedom, but because the foundation of each prison he has been to is the same: It is a place where people are caged like shelter dogs, where they are identified by a number or by "Inmate!," and where violence and cruelty manifest often.

Ivan's experiences at San Quentin and New Folsom were especially telling. San Quentin is almost beautiful, its sand-colored walls jetting out into the San Francisco Bay, its guard tower positioned like a lighthouse against the postcard backdrop of the Richmond–San Rafael Bridge. With easy access to Northern California's hotbeds of progressive activism—Berkeley, Oakland, and San Francisco—the prison offers several programs from art workshops to college classes, and frequently welcomes guest speakers from organizations like Human Rights Watch and the American Civil Liberties Union. A revamped recording studio has allowed podcasts like *Ear Hustle* (recorded using a hybrid of incarcerated and outside hosts and production crews) to become mainstream entertainment. *Ear Hustle* was even nominated for a Pulitzer Prize and earned its original incarcerated host, Earlonne Woods, a sentence commutation from the governor.[1]

Conversely, California State Prison Sacramento, known more commonly as New Folsom, has very few programs for people seeking creative outlets or higher education; it is known mostly for its violent history. In 2021 the FBI opened a probe into a coordinated effort between guards and the Aryan Brotherhood—a white-supremacist prison gang—to murder three prisoners.[2] Riots in 1996 and 2011 left one incarcerated man killed and a fifteen people injured.[3] Ivan was incarcerated at New Folsom when Hugo Pinell, who participated in the alleged escape attempt that led to the fatal shooting of Black revolutionary activist and author George Jackson, was killed during a 2015 riot.[4]

What's important to keep in mind, Ivan explains, is that this juxtaposition between San Quentin and New Folsom does not make the former a "good" prison. Programming at San Quentin has routinely been stripped away for minor infractions—such as smoking a cigarette, stepping across a yellow line, or using the telephone too long—indicating, Ivan says, that rehabilitation is an excuse for prison, not its purpose. If prisons were meant to rehabilitate, why would infractions lead to *less* programming? Why would a person need to serve a life sentence? The real purpose of prison, he believes, is to deny the humanity and existence of certain members of society, to hide them away in plain sight. At the end of the day, the professors and organizers leave, and the men return to cold cells and an environment defined by dehumanization and violence. San Quentin, Ivan says, is not a "good" prison, because there is no such thing as a good prison. It is designed, like all the others, to dehumanize, destabilize, and deactivate.

This was no more apparent than in 2020 when San Quentin became an epicenter of one of the worst coronavirus outbreaks in the country; reckless actions taken by the prison department exemplified the type of dehumanization that defines incarceration. In May that year, administrators ordered a transfer of prisoners from California Institution for Men into San Quentin, a technique the department has used for years to get around a federal mandate ordering the administration to decarcerate its dangerously overcrowded facilities. Before the transfer, San Quentin had zero cases of COVID-19 among its population. California Institution for Men had already had an outbreak, and prison administrators insisted the transferees not be tested before they boarded the bus. Within three months of the transfer, 2,237 prisoners at San Quentin became infected with the virus, the most of any facility at that time. Twenty-nine incarcerated men died as a result.[5]

The carelessness with which prison administrators and staff were treating the potential for the novel coronavirus to devastate the prison population was already well documented by the time the San Quentin transfer took place—in large part thanks to footage Ivan had captured on his cell phone. (Although considered prison contraband, hundreds of thousands of cell phones are smuggled inside, usually by guards.) Aired by Vice News in April 2020, the video shows groups of men working out and congregating in groups inside the dormitory, with yard time limited or, in some prisons, prohibited due to the pandemic lockdown. There are no barriers, no protective face coverings.

"All it takes is just one person in here to become infected with the coronavirus, and it's a wrap," Ivan told Vice. "Everyone's going to be infected."[6]

The video received half a million views, and almost immediately reporters began tracking down footage from prisons around the country. These morbid videos captured men dying in their cells and prisoners provided with inadequate protective measures, such as a hotel-sized bar of soap distributed every other week. The truth about COVID inside prisons was out, and emergency decarceration methods were taken by several states, proving the viability of decarceration on a large scale.

In the meantime, Solano had it out for Ivan. Vice neglected to alter his voice in the interview, and it was clear who the source of the video had been. Guards tossed Ivan's cell looking for the phone. When they came up empty, they tossed the cells of the prisoners Ivan had filmed, telling them Ivan was to blame for lost privileges such as exercise and day-room activity time. The hope was, of course, that retribution would take care of the administration's PR problem. But when the men saw the video, and the changes the administration began to make as a result of it—all of a sudden, masks and soap were more readily available—Ivan was given a reprieve.

That's not to say prison is easy for Ivan, and the first time he speaks to a new batch of interns for his nonprofit, he implores them to think beyond making prison a better place.

"A prison is an inhumane place, and nothing can alter the existing structure enough to change that," he said to a group of UC Irvine students. "Please. Don't waste my time trying to make it more comfortable for me in here."

"We Don't Play with Black Kids"

Ivan grew up in Wewoka, Oklahoma, a small farm town in Seminole territory about an hour east of Oklahoma City. The town was established in 1849 as a Black Seminole settlement at a time when most Indigenous people were getting displaced and pushed west. Wewoka's foundation as a haven for Black Indigenous people was solidified by generations of families who stayed in the area and raised their families there. When Ivan was growing up, it was an almost entirely Black neighborhood, surrounded by almost entirely white suburbs. Ivan didn't think about race until he started attending a local elementary school with kids from the white part of town.

"I remember this white kid saying, 'Hey, we don't play with Black kids,' and I was just like, 'Okay, what's a Black kid?'"

Like past revolutionaries—George Jackson, Marcus Garvey, and others—Ivan became radicalized starting with these early feelings of otherness. In a letter to Bantam Books editor Greg Armstrong, Jackson described it thusly:

> We played and fought on the corner sidewalks bordering the school. "They" had a large grass-and-tree-studded garden with an eight-foot wrought-iron fence bordering it (to keep us out, since it never seemed to keep any of them in when they chose to leave).[7]

This practice of *othering*, as coined by UC Berkeley's john a. powell, may seem remote to some readers, but it is a common experience among most people.

"When we pretend we're not connected, we're in the process of othering," said powell—who spells his name with lowercase letters to be "part of the universe, not over it, as capitals signify"—at a keynote address for Berkeley's Othering & Belonging Institute, where he serves as director. "We're in the process of denying not only someone's humanity, but our own humanity, and denying our connectedness."[8]

Ivan felt disconnected from his peers both physically and emotionally. He lived very distinctly on the other side of the tracks from his white classmates. His teachers used racial slurs, and the more he defied them, the more escalated the conflict between himself and authority figures became.

"It started to fester in me, not only as a distrust of society but also as an anger that kept me constantly in the principal's office," Ivan said. "I'm getting sent to the office as early as the second and third grade for not saying the Pledge of Allegiance, and I'm like, 'How am I gonna go pledge allegiance to the flag when my teacher's calling me a n——?'"

Ivan chronicled glimpses of his childhood in his book, *Mayhem, Murder & Magnificence: A Memoir*, one of four he self-published during his incarceration. In his reflections, his interpersonal experiences as a child become increasingly infused by race, as the adults in his life provide him with different ways to interpret his place in society as a young Black man. His teachers firmly placed him on the bottom rung of a racial hierarchy Ivan wasn't even aware of until he entered school. His grandfather instilled in him a deep mistrust of white people, a belief system rooted in the experience of being disowned by Ivan's great-grandmother, a Native American, on account of the "Negro blood" he inherited from Ivan's great-grandfather. Ivan's grandmother, on the other hand, "accepted her place" in the racial hierarchy, according to her grandson's memoir, earning a low but steady income cleaning houses with a "yes, sir" and "no, ma'am" disposition that harkened from another time.

These mixed messages around racial identity from his family and teachers manifested in Ivan a complex mentality that would ultimately shape his future.

"The mannish boy would quickly grow into a reserved man," Ivan wrote. "And yet, before he could accomplish anything, there was the instability, impulsiveness, and lack of self-esteem he would have to encounter and conquer."[9]

Ivan's aunt Betty remembers a sweet and smart child who had to grow up quickly. Ivan's father was murdered when he was three. Ivan's mother remarried and quickly became overwhelmed with stepchildren and a worsening drug addiction. His grandparents, who raised Ivan and his sisters, grew infirm by the time he was in high school. Ivan, Aunt Betty said, became a "mother hen" to his sisters and increasingly ill grandparents. He started earning money as a landscaper when he was ten years old, but it was grueling work. When a friend told him he could make $40 in a single night, he was easily persuaded to trade in his gardening tools.

It was 1987, and Ivan was thirteen. A man named Preston Reese had opened up the first crack house in the neighborhood. With the US crack epidemic in full swing, and inner-city Black communities acutely impacted by it, Reese's establishment quickly became a hotspot. He offered to pay Ivan and his friend to act as lookouts. As the boys proved themselves trustworthy, they were given small amounts of crack to sell to local users. Always a student, Ivan learned the mechanics of the crack trade—manufacturing, distribution, and security—and by the time he was twenty he was trafficking drugs between Oklahoma and California.

Ivan describes his first prison sentence as an almost natural consequence of being a young Black man swept up in the 1980s crack boom. Studies have shown that violence escalated quickly in communities shortly after the crack trade entered; the murder rate of young Black males doubled soon after the drug came on scene. Although the majority of young Black men were not directly involved in the crack market, an increased presence of guns and profit wars spread like a virus in these communities, putting residents in one of two categories: participants or collateral damage.[10] As a participant, Ivan said, he lived by a strict code of loyalty and a kill-or-be-killed mentality.

"I don't want to make excuses and put it all off on race, but it definitely plays a factor," Ivan told me. "As a young Black man, I didn't have people telling me I could conquer the world, that I could go out there and be anything I wanted it to be. So we believed that drug dealing or robbery was the way, and that was constantly reinforced by the need to get by any means necessary. And necessity knows no law."

In 1995 a friend he trusted and relied on broke into Ivan's family home. His world was destabilized and his protective nature went into overdrive, with his wife, mother, and sisters all living under the roof of the property. Ivan confronted the man the following week at a party, and when the meeting got heated, Ivan shot and killed him. After Ivan's trial ended in a hung jury, he pled guilty to first-degree manslaughter and spent the next four years in Oklahoma's prison system, two in the Seminole County Jail and two at Cimarron City Correctional Facility. When he was paroled in 1998, he got as far from Oklahoma as he could, determined to start over fresh in California.

Agency

Ivan founded United Black Family Scholarship Foundation, a non-profit organization, from a California maximum security cell in 2014.

It was a year after he completed the 300-plus-page manuscript for his first book, *Domestic Genocide: The Institutionalization of Society*, a labor of love typed up on a banged-up computer—the kind that used floppy disks—that he was allowed to access for one hour each day. He had the disk smuggled out and the book published in 2013. Then he was thrown into the security housing unit.

When Ivan emerged, his world had become something of a blank canvas. The department had transferred him to Salinas Valley State Prison, some 200 miles from his previous facility in Sacramento. In the supermax sector, contraband phones were going at a rate far beyond Ivan's means at the time, so web surfing and social networking were off the table. His magnum opus completed and in print, he began seeking a new outlet for his creative energy. One day his cellie walked in with a massive hardcover book detailing how to start a nonprofit, and Ivan realized his next venture had just found him.

He proceeded to learn about documentation, the required governance structure, and associated fees of filing for a 501(c)(3). He drew up articles of incorporation and sought out his three initial directors, one of the requirements for establishing a nonprofit. He started with people close to him on the outside, making phone calls to two friends from Oakland and his cousin Darryl.

Darryl was skeptical. The boys had grown up together in Oklahoma, and Darryl's memories of Ivan were stained with his criminal activities and interactions with law enforcement. His initial reaction to Ivan's proposal that Darryl serve as a director for the nonprofit was, according to Ivan, "C'mon, cuz. You've been in so much shit, and you want me to sign up with you on some nonprofit so I end up in the pen, too?" It may not have been the answer he wanted, but Ivan had come to terms with the man he presented to the world prior to his incarceration by way of the self-reflection he made in *Domestic Genocide*. So he sent Darryl a copy. Soon afterward, the cousins reconnected on the phone.

"He said, 'You sure have changed, ain't you?'" Ivan recalled. "He was still hesitant to get caught up in anything so I said, 'Cuz, you've known me my whole life and you know I've always been a man of my word. If you sign on, you have my word that everything I do from here on out is on the level.'"

Ivan sent directorial forms to the two men in Oakland and Darryl, who aggregated the forms, the documents of incorporation Ivan had completed, and the $40 filing fee, and sent it to Oklahoma's secretary of state. The department responded with additional information that was needed to complete the application, as well as a copy of the state penal code that bars any incarcerated person from holding an executive role at a nonprofit. Ivan was ready for this final obstacle: Darryl had agreed to act as his power of attorney.

Since then, the organization has taken on projects such as funding a local youth basketball team in Oklahoma and publishing works by incarcerated authors. Ivan's community-based revolution is detailed in grant letters for the nonprofit's REBUILD program, an acronym for Reinvest in Every Black and Underserved Institution to Liberate and Diversify. (Gotta love nonprofits and their acronyms.) The program is designed to engage community members in neighborhood revitalization projects to disrupt the poverty-to-prison and school-to-prison pipelines. Grant documents for REBUILD detail how homes, schools, and neighborhood amenities will be reconstructed, updated, and developed by the people who will live, learn, and work in the area—thereby manifesting an investment in maintaining its safety and integrity.

"A lot of criminal justice nonprofits are catching the problem [of mass incarceration] by the tail, dealing with a lot of reform issues for people already in prison," Ivan explained. "We're saying, 'Hold up, let's address issues on the *front* end. Let's have a program that's working to stop the induction of people going into the prison system, as opposed to working with people once they're in there or after they come out.' That's like focusing efforts on things that are the symptoms, not the root problem."

It's a strategy that has been embraced by abolitionist thought leaders like Zach Norris, former executive director of the Ella Baker

Center for Human Rights, who explored the idea of a society without prisons in his book *Defund Fear: Safety without Policing, Prisons, and Punishment.* "In a comprehensive new system of public safety, we must move from punishment to accountability, from deprivation to resources, from suspicion to relationships, and from isolation to participation," Norris writes.[11]

Ivan can attest to the effectiveness of putting blood, sweat, and tears into building a community from personal experience. After paroling to Oakland from Oklahoma, he got a job working in construction. Jerry Brown, who had just won the mayoral race, had proposed a "revitalization" of downtown Oakland, a series of construction projects and an injection of private enterprise that would increase the quality of life for residents and buoy the economy. The plan included 10,000 refurbished residences for the area, earning the project the title the 10K Plan. Ivan became a foreman for one of the development sites, a position that made him feel invested in the look, upkeep, and well-being of the neighborhood. He got to know the tenants who lived there; he carried groceries for elderly residents; he showed up at 4:30 a.m. to sweep trash from the streets.

"Years later, when I'm thinking about putting this organization together, I thought about those memorable moments, of how I was able to connect to that community," Ivan said. "I was able to take a certain level of pride in the community."

But the 10K Plan stripped away any hope Ivan and his working-class peers had for becoming a part of the new downtown coterie. The modernized units were priced far above what the average worker living in Oakland could afford, which led to a vast gentrification that pushed many of downtown's former residents, and certainly the workers who revitalized it, to East Oakland or into tent cities. According to local activists, no affordable housing units would have been built without the organized community protests at that time.[12]

This result is not unique to Oakland. Most neighborhoods selected for government-funded improvements end up being gentrified, with the original residents pushed farther away from city centers.

"Revitalization does generally occur when a neighborhood becomes attractive to the middle class, but all too often the gentrification that follows does not include strict enforcement of inclusionary zoning principles, and it gradually drives the African American poor out of their now-upgraded neighborhoods and into newly segregated inner-ring suburbs," writes Rothstein.[13]

Ivan's collective participation in developing downtown meant he felt invested, but denial of agency within downtown—the fact that he couldn't afford to live there—thrust him into a common cycle. He and his coworkers had built the doors that were now closing in their faces. He looked for work, but he'd light up criminal background checks and be rebuffed. He tried something more entrepreneurial, but he lacked the kind of equity he needed as startup capital.

"At one point, I wanted to open an urban clothing store, but the bank told me I needed to put down fifty grand just to get going," Ivan said. "At that point in my life, I only knew one way to make that kind of money."

Again, the effects of othering were upon him. As Norris writes, "The less agency you're able to exercise in your life, because of complex, intractable systems, the more likely you are to embrace the idea of an external enemy you can blame."[14]

Ivan blamed the capitalist system seemingly intent on denying him, so he went back to what he saw as the only way he could make ends meet: selling drugs. It hadn't changed much. The demand was great, the money was ample, and the relationships were still marred with violent undertones. Ivan says one man in particular, William Anderson, repeatedly attacked him and robbed him on several occasions. On July 16, 2000, Ivan was ready to return fire. He shot and killed Anderson and was sentenced to life without the possibility of parole, a flowery term for death by incarceration.

"So where did it all go wrong," he'd ponder from his prison cell years later. As he reflected on his experience in Oakland, he began writing the specs for the REBUILD program. He pinpointed the defects of Brown's 10K Plan that had thrown his life in reverse; he designed the REBUILD neighborhoods to be developed by the people who reside there—and will continue to live there post-revitalization. He thought about access to capital and included training programs that would allow participants to assist in the revitalization while also ensuring they acquired skills to earn a living wage. The parameters for qualifying neighborhoods were high concentrations of dilapidated homes and high incarceration rates, neighborhoods like the one he grew up in.

The pilot REBUILD neighborhood is in the Eastside neighborhood of Oklahoma City, about seventy miles west of Wewoka. Using public databases, student interns have identified 1,200 neglected properties within a fifteen-mile radius. As of autumn 2023, volunteers were planning onboarding processes, holding workshops for community members on basic trade skills like carpentry and plumbing. By creating stability in housing, marketable skills, and a livable wage, the program will interrupt the revolving door of Black and Brown people filing into prison, and abolition is attained by starving the system of bodies.

"We provide community members and young adults with opportunities and resources to build life skills and job skills, develop economic stability, and escape the grasp of the school-to-prison pipeline," Ivan said. "Our work is designed to 'rebuild the community from within the community.'"

What (or Who) Is Broken?

To pave the road of his revolution, Ivan has enlisted the help of a younger generation. Like the liberation movements he learned about from elders while sitting in the Alameda County jail, such as the Black Panther Party and the Free Speech Movement, Ivan's strategy relies primarily on the hunger, resilience, and curiosity of college students. These students serve as interns, and each cohort is focused on one element of Ivan's blueprint for a reimagined future.

The same year he arrived at Salinas, 2014, the California legislature had passed Senate Bill 1391, removing an obstacle erected in the

1970s that prevented community colleges from receiving compensation for teaching courses inside carceral settings. As luck would have it, Salinas was one of the first facilities to start offering college courses. Ivan signed up for a sociology course taught by Professor Megan McNamara.

"I signed up with a plan, specifically to open a doorway to engage with students," Ivan said. "I didn't really give a shit about sociology, I knew that stuff like the back of my hand." At that time he was always carrying around *Domestic Genocide*, his pride and joy. One day after class, he slipped a copy into the teacher's backpack. The following week, she asked Ivan if he'd lecture her class of students at UC Santa Cruz.

Ivan maintained a rapport with Megan over the years, regularly participating as a presenter or a student in her classes. In 2019 a group of UC Santa Cruz undergraduates under Megan's tutelage signed up to be the first intern cohort at UBFSF. That same year, the organization raised enough funds to fly the entire group to Oklahoma City for a conference regarding the REBUILD project. Attendees were met by Glenn E. Martin, an entrepreneur and activist who founded the campaign CLOSErikers to close New York City's main jail complex, and former state senator Connie Johnson. These feature guests led the students in a series of leadership training sessions and walked them through neighborhoods they'd previously identified for potential revitalization.

"If you've ever planned a conference before, try adding on an element of sitting in a prison cell on top of everything else that could go wrong," said Glenn, who spent six years imprisoned in New York and now consults with social justice nonprofits across the country through his entrepreneurial endeavor GEM Trainers. As of 2023 he also sits on the board of United Black Family Scholarship Foundation. "The fact that he was able to plan this conference, motivate these volunteers, including a former state senator, to show up, to participate, to share their gifts was really impressive to me, to be quite honest."

Since the pilot internship program, Ivan's organization has penned additional agreements with groups at UC Berkeley, UC Irvine, Stony

Brook University, and Langston University. Ivan meets with each cohort, either by prerecording a video or via a prison-issued tablet. After the introductory meeting, they are guided by volunteers— usually university professors or teaching assistants—who train them in grant writing, data collection, or whatever skill set is needed for their particular assignment.

The UC Irvine students, for example, were seeking out and applying for grants to fund the REBUILD project. I sat in on the introductory session and watched as students popped into the virtual meeting one at a time, seemingly busy with other goings-on in their screen-filled lives. When Ivan connected—his face warm and welcoming against a backdrop of cold, harsh walls—all eyes were transfixed on him.

He's come to embrace this kind of reaction.

"It creates a space where we can have very authentic conversations about what prison does to families and individuals, and how change can be effected through their efforts," he told me afterward.

The meeting started with round-robin sharing, each student saying why they had chosen an internship with UBFSF over more traditional, trade-based opportunities, ones you might see at a job fair. The usual array of reformist buzzwords echoed in the corner of my kitchen where I sat listening in:

"I just think the criminal justice system is broken and we need to fix it," said a soft-spoken young man, his eyes never looking directly at the camera.

"Is it, though?" pressed Ivan. "'Cause from where I'm sitting . . ." He paused to look around at his surroundings, drawing attention to the lack of good lighting and the prison-labor-manufactured furniture. ". . . it's working just the way it's supposed to. It's silencing a generation of voters who could threaten the establishment. I'd like y'all to think about that for a second."

One by one, the students shared their desire to make a difference, and one by one, Ivan challenged them to think beyond the usual course of protest and reform. In this first meeting, he didn't mention abolition by name, but he did start leading the flock toward it.

"It only seems logical that if we're going to make a change, it starts with the next generation, because they're the ones coming in on the coattails of our ideas and building on them," Ivan said. "If we look at the history of revolutionary movements, they all got their start on college campuses, probably because—and I quote Frederick Douglass when I say—'It is much easier to build with strong children as opposed to broken men.'"

Whenever Ivan mentions the Douglass quote, which he does quite often, I think about Malcolm X, specifically the black-and-white image of him standing in front of the window, rifle at the ready, peeking through the curtains. He knows that the police won't protect him and the world is out to get him, not just the FBI under J. Edgar Hoover—probably the greatest all-time example of white supremacy infecting law enforcement—not just the violent racists, but his community of Black Muslims, infiltrated and corrupted by the aforementioned police. He is fighting against a system that has pegged him to be a violent man, an image he has refuted both by his general demeanor and his religious devotion, and here he stands with a gun that reaches from his hip socket to the top of the doorframe. Imagine waking up one day with all the answers, knowing all the steps between where you are and where you belong, grabbing your gun, and carefully drawing back the curtain to see if today is the day you are going to die. How could that not break someone?

People talk about the criminal legal system being broken, but as Ivan told the students, that's not entirely accurate. The heinous scenes of police brutality we find so shocking on the nightly news are what abolitionist Mariame Kaba calls the "logical result of policing in America."[15] (Kaba founded Project NIA, another abolitionist organization that focuses on juvenile justice and community-based alternatives to formal legal proceedings.) The system is working just as it was designed to work.

Rather, it is we who are broken, a society crushed under the moral weight of never fully accounting for our history of enslaving our fellow humans; under centuries of state-sponsored execution, civil death, and prison labor. Kaba talks about this phenomenon in terms of "systems that live within us, that manifest outside of us."[16]

I recognize this manifestation in my own life. For years, I played little league baseball under New York City's Robert F. Kennedy Bridge on a small islet known as Randall's Island. Looming large just over a mile across the East River from Randall's Island is Rikers Island, the 413-acre home to New York City's main jail complex. The island is named after Richard Riker, who served as the recorder of New York City for three consecutive terms and was a member of the "Kidnapping Club," a group that would capture freed slaves and sell them back to Southerners in the 1830s.[17] In the age of mass incarceration, Rikers has developed a reputation similar to that of its namesake: violent and cruel. In 2008 guards ran a prisoner fight club that ultimately led to the death of eighteen-year-old Christopher Robinson. It only got worse from there; prisoner injuries doubled (from 15,620 to 31,368) between 2008 and 2017, even as the population declined 32 percent. Since 2016, there has been a 105 percent increase in use-of-force incidents by New York City correctional officers at Rikers against people in their custody.[18]

"When it comes to ignominies, New York City's island jail complex has it all: inmate violence, staff brutality, rape, abuse of adolescents and the mentally ill, and one of the nation's highest rates of solitary confinement," stated a 2013 *Mother Jones* article ranking Rikers as one of America's ten worst prisons. "Yet the East River island remains a dismal and dangerous place for the 12,000 or more men, women, and children held there on any given day—mostly pretrial defendants who can't make bail and nonviolent offenders with sentences too short to ship them upstate."[19]

This torture tomb was the backdrop to my childhood Saturdays on the dirt fields of Randall's.

My brokenness, my internalization of oppressive systems, is reflected in the fact that I don't remember seeing it. Mind you, this is a monstrous

facility that I would have had a direct line of sight to from my position
at shortstop. Perhaps I wouldn't have understood the concept of crime
and punishment at that age, but I didn't even think to ask. The adoring
parent fans didn't seem to take notice of it or attempt to shield us from
it, so it simply faded into obscurity amid the winding roadways and
railways connecting Queens, Manhattan, and the Bronx. When I fly
into New York today, it's the first thing I notice as we approach JFK, this
sprawling complex of X-shaped buildings and barbed wire interrupting
the calm flow of the East River on its way out to sea.

"As a society, we have long turned away from any social concern
that overwhelms us," Kaba writes. "Whether it's war, climate change,
or the prison industrial complex, Americans have been conditioned to
simply look away from profound harms."[20]

In fact, this is the brokenness Frederick Douglass may have
intended to expose. The quote Ivan references is frequently attributed
to Douglass, but it hasn't been traced back to any of his known works.
The closest thing is a paragraph in his 1855 slave narrative *My Bondage
and My Freedom*, in which he writes:

> When I went into [Master Hugh's] family, it was the abode of hap-
> piness and contentment. The mistress of the house was a model of
> affection and tenderness. . . . She had bread for the hungry, clothes
> for the naked, and comfort for every mourner that came within her
> reach. Slavery soon proved its ability to divest her of these excellent
> qualities, and her home of its early happiness. Conscience cannot
> stand much violence. Once thoroughly broken down, who is he
> that can repair the damage? It may be broken toward the slave, on
> Sunday, and toward the master on Monday.[21]

Considering prisons and jails are where we hide away, or "disap-
pear," thousands of people a year, the facilities themselves are quite
prominent. They are hidden in plain sight, surrounded by large cities,
or alongside major highways. And yet they might as well be invisible.
We gloss over them, our brokenness allowing us to operate with clear
consciences by denying their existence.

The Prisoner's Legacy

Of the two of us, Ivan would be the broken one, you'd think, having spent the majority of his life at the mercy of an institution designed to break him. But his resilience is undeniable, a common characteristic, according to Glenn, of people who serve time.

"I quickly realized in prison that if you stop living and just wait, life is what happens while you're doing that," Glenn said. "To be successful in prison you need to figure out how to live given your new reality, and it's part of what makes people who've been in prison so resilient.

"I don't think that Black folks and Brown folks and poor people ask for that as a way to become resilient," he continued. "I would have preferred a gap year."

Ivan's resilience is buoyed by an incredible sense of humor. He laughs off his situation often and can dish it as well as he can take it. Never one to back down from a good ol' fashioned battle of the wits, I once busted his chops for being a "diva" about wanting his full name in a video I'd made from one of our interviews. (I had used his first initial in case prison administrators ran a search.) He paid me back by answering one of my calls with the cadence of a voicemail recording.

"Hello. You've reached the voicemail of Ivan Kilgore."

The imitation was so convincing that I hung up. He called back howling.

"Who got jokes now?!" he exclaimed with glee.

"That's very Ivan-esque," said Glenn when I relayed the story. "I mean where do you find that sense of humor in the middle of a factory of despair? Where do you find the ability to find joy in life in a place that is meant to take away your joy?"

Ivan says his sense of humor developed from his survival instincts: Being treated like target practice for verbal strikes from guards, he learned to cope by laughing it off or turning the jab into a meaningless barb by creating a comedic dialogue out of the interaction. He's honed this skill so acutely that he seamlessly integrates humor into more serious, heavy conversations. Once when we were talking about the pains of trying to assimilate into the racial hierarchy he grew up with, he said, "And I never did it real well, neither. Probably why I'm sitting in a prison cell." He laughed and permitted me to do so as well.

I've only heard Ivan despondent once. He had mentioned his daughter in passing, and I realized we had never spoken about her at length. He had a child when he was living in Oakland. He'd fallen back into the drug game to support her and her mother, and he'd been sent to prison when she was very young. We had never gone in-depth about his role as a parent. I asked him to tell me about their relationship.

"Man, that's a rough thing to talk about right now," he said solemnly.

Ivan's daughter, at that point, hadn't spoken to him in over a year. According to her father, she had sought some financial help and, when Ivan tried to convince her to build something she could profit from long-term, she rebuffed him. She was looking for money, not advice from someone spending their life in prison.

"As a father, I want to provide some guidance and direction for my child, but because of my incarceration, my influence in her life is limited to letters, short phone calls, and such," Ivan said. "I'll try to teach her some of the lessons I've learned and she'll be like, 'You've been gone my whole life. How are you gonna start showing me something now?'"

Ivan's fraught relationship with his only descendant complicated his thoughts on legacy when we first started talking. He recalled a writing workshop at New Folsom prison that offered a prompt about how each man would want to be remembered. It forced Ivan to look back on his past and reconcile it with his present, not as a prisoner but as a man with ambitions of bettering the society that had perceived him as a threat.

"People who focus on legacy, they're not consumed with the world and life as it is, but more so how they're going to leave it and the impression that they leave on it," Ivan said. "I don't want people to remember me for being a young drug dealer, someone who was, you know, quick to enforce violence when it came to defending mine. That just doesn't sit right with me.

"I'm a convicted felon, but that doesn't mean I don't have value in this society. I have more value in society *because* of my experiences in prison."

The idea of legacy also prompted him to start thinking outside the box—and beyond prison walls—in terms of ways he could exert influence, not only on his daughter but on the greater community of Black men. He does this both through the programs he designs around neighborhood revitalization and by mentoring young men with whom he crosses paths inside prison. He is now the elder teaching revolutionary lessons about Black Power movements, focusing on programs like the Black Panther food banks that exemplified the power of investing in the community.

He also relays life lessons he learned as a child working on his grandfather's farm.

"When you cultivate the soil and you plant the seeds and you nourish those seeds, you produce what you need to sustain life," he said. "When we think about our youth in these communities, what we're not doing is cultivating the soil. The soil is stagnated with blood and bullets. We gotta make sure that kids at those key points in their lives have those stable environments and mentors to keep them on the right track."

As he's worked to redefine his life, his daughter has pivoted as well and now works alongside him as an administrator for UBFSF. The idea of running a "family business" tickles Ivan, grateful that he has made progress in how he'll be remembered and stunned at the improbability of the turn his life has taken.

America has never made good on its promises of life, liberty, and happiness to people like Ivan. Rejected by banks, and shut out of revitalized neighborhoods, the country's economic and political systems have consistently denied him access, mobility, and choice. The criminal legal system has served to isolate him from society, label him as an unacceptable other, and cast him into a life of solitude. Still, he reaches back, developing research papers to better cities where he'll probably never live—or even set foot in—educating students who will

likely never shake his hand or thank him in person, and building relationships with professors in whose classrooms he will likely never sit.

"When you're in the middle of the storm and it's really dark, it's
easy to forget that there's light up ahead," said Glenn. "It feels like Ivan
wakes up every day and walks towards that light, light that he can't
even see."

Sister by Gerald Morgan

4

Reimagining Justice:
Critical Resistance

On the corner of 44th and Telegraph is the bright blue brick-and-mortar offices of Critical Resistance, a modern abolitionist organization founded by feminist icon Angela Davis, carceral geographer Ruth Wilson Gilmore, and environmental and human liberation activist Rose Braz in the late 1990s. It's a relatively new property for the organization, which was previously headquartered closer to downtown Oakland. When I visited in the fall of 2021, wood support beams were still stabilizing the hollowed-out interior. The building previously housed a baby store, a seemingly perfect fit for an organization dedicated to outfitting the next generation of freedom fighters with tools for success.

On approach, the first thing to catch your eye is a mantra above the front entrance: "Building People *Power*." "People" is written in yellow, embossed letters, the other two words in white; "power" being italicized emphasizes the different ways the phrase can be read. The windows facing Telegraph Avenue serve as frames for large posters displaying photographs of volunteers and pamphlets devoted to the organization's various campaigns. Along the 44th Street side of the building are murals, not necessarily unique to this part of town where young artists frequently fill the night air with spray paint to leave their mark on the city. Street art is prolific here, as it is in many major cities, and after George Floyd was killed by police in 2020, portraits of him and other victims of police homicide blanketed the boarded-up retail shops along Broadway from the Bay to Lake Merritt. The downtown area became an outside exhibition of art, culture, and resistance.

The Critical Resistance building captures this juxtaposition of beauty and pain on its façade by surrounding revolutionary quotes with elegant imagery. Bold orange flowers and butterflies frame a four-panel window containing summaries of the organization's successful battles against gang injunctions, the Urban Shield weapons exposition, and the construction of what would have been the state's thirty-fourth prison, Delano II. The silhouettes of two birds stretch out a banner spelling out the organization's three-part theory of change: "Dismantle, Change, Build." Next to the window is the figure of an African American woman, the crown of her head breaching the concrete line where the wall meets the sidewalk like a sunrise. Her eyes gaze upward at a white dove she's just released from her hands, outstretched from the ground. The dove flies up and seemingly aims to arrive at the word "Libertad," spelled out in golden block letters. It stretches over a metal roll-up gate featuring a quote from Frantz Fanon: "When we revolt it's not for a particular culture. We revolt simply because, for many reasons, we can no longer breathe." A woman, painted in a purple hue, blows into a conch shell, inflating the *D* in "Libertad." Orange and yellow rings radiate from her skyward-facing forehead, a long braid sweeping her profile and resting along the bottom edge of the wall.

On the day of my visit, Critical Resistance (CR) was holding its monthly Freedom Friday, a free outdoor event, open to the public, featuring music, food, and activities. Mohamed Shehk, the group's national campaigns and programs director, said CR launched

Freedom Fridays back in the fall of 2020, shortly after purchasing the new property. The idea was to build community by breaking bread and having conversations with neighborhood residents. Central to CR's modus operandi, according to all the staffers I spoke to, is the organization's maintenance of its role as a facilitator of change, not a prescriber. Every plan for change starts with a conversation. New systems are defined by building relationships and learning from members of the community where CR is operating. At the front lines of all the organization does are the people who will be most directly impacted by whatever change it is trying to bring about.

"We never helicopter in solutions," said one staff member.

Freedom Fridays are also an opportunity to highlight some of the many organizations CR works with. As part of its mission to "build people power," CR participates in several coalitions of similarly missioned nonprofits and advocacy groups. Because CR is one of the oldest grassroots organizations in the area, it uses its notoriety to uplift lesser-known local groups. On this particular Friday in September, with children recently returning to school from summer break, members of the Education for Liberation Coalition were promoting a textbook-size compendium designed to help educators and parents draw connections between educational practices and the growing abolition movement. *Lessons in Liberation: An Abolitionist Toolkit for Educators* is the result of a partnership between CR's editorial collective and Quetzal Education Consulting, a nonprofit working to integrate abolitionist and anti-racist philosophies into education policy.

"Part of the reason why we prioritize coalition work is anchored in our orientation towards movement building," said Woods Ervin, a longtime CR member who joined the staff as the national media and communications director in 2022. "Our priority is to shift power towards communities, so that means working with several organizations with members who are directly impacted by a particular aspect of the prison industrial complex that we've decided to fight."

The prison-industrial complex, or PIC, is the Final Boss in CR's quest to dismantle oppressive systems. One of Critical Resistance's most prominent campaigns, and the reason for my visit, is its involvement in the Close California Prisons coalition. The group includes staffers from Californians United for a Responsible Budget (CURB), Californians for Safety and Justice, Showing Up for Racial Justice, California Coalition for Women Prisoners, and Dignity and Power Now. Their goal is for the governor to account for ten prison closures—either complete or forthcoming—in the state's 2025 budget.

The coalition has been together since CURB released *The People's Plan for Prison Closure* in 2021. The People's Plan outlines several problems associated with the prison system, including environmental dangers like water toxicity, the economic strain on both the state and the cities where the prisons are located, and threats to public health. Based on these parameters, the CURB report suggested ten prisons that should be closed immediately: California Rehabilitation Center, Kern Valley State Prison, Pleasant Valley State Prison, California Correctional Institution, North Kern State Prison, California Substance Abuse Treatment Facility, California State Prison Los Angeles County, California Medical Facility, Avenal State Prison, and California Men's Colony. Deuel Vocational Institution has already been shuttered, and two more are slated for closure before 2025: the California Correctional Center and Chuckawalla Valley State Prison.[1]

One might wonder why organizations fighting for the rights of incarcerated individuals would list a "rehabilitation center," a "substance abuse treatment facility," and a "medical facility," but note that these misnomers are attempts to portray the prison department as an empathetic party. This stands in stark contrast to reality, being that prison's central purpose, as we examined in chapter 2, is to punish and incapacitate. It should be noted that the California Rehabilitation Center can't even seem to rehabilitate *itself*—its infrastructure and medical facilities are in such disarray even after millions of taxpayer dollars had been poured into it that it was slated for closure several times between 2010 and 2020. Many of these facilities provide insufficient medical care and are mere fronts the prison department can use to shuffle prisoners around rather than lower the population through releases.

Connected Liberation

A few days after the Freedom Friday event, CR staffers Viju Mathew and Isa Borgeson walked me through how they campaign for shut-downs in prison towns. By chance, we met on the same day the Deuel Vocational Institution, a state prison located in unincorporated San Joaquin County, began a so-called warm shutdown. The prison was slated for closure, but having presented no plan for safely shut-ting down, CDCR negotiated to have the prisoners transferred (not released) to other facilities and for the prison to remain operating at 50 percent, which keeps about half the staff employed for the pur-poses of overseeing basic plumbing, electrical, and water treatment operations.[2] It was far from ideal, but spirits were still high among the three of us.

While Deuel was not part of CURB's initial assessment of highly problematic complexes, the facility was an easy choice for the gov-ernor: The prison had an annual operating cost of $182 million and needed a reported $800 million in repairs. Additionally, toxic water from the prison had been poisoning the streams that feed into the Sacramento–San Joaquin Delta.[3] For purely economic and environ-mental reasons, the prison had become more of a liability than the state had bargained for.

"I think when we understand prisons as a public health crisis, as an environmental crisis, when you think about the fires that are happening just miles out of reach of people potentially being burned alive, the conversation shifts," Isa said. "Between that and the prison population being lower than it has been in many years, the opportu-nity is being presented to act now to close these prisons."

Having grown up in an activist family—both of her parents were involved in the protests in the Philippines following Ferdinand Mar-cos's declaration of martial law and the human rights abuses that followed—Isa was politicized early on in her life, but her radicalization toward abolition came in 2007 when a close family member was sent to prison. The family member, who had been involved with Critical Resistance before his incarceration, started teaching Isa about organizing and abolition work. She formed relationships with other people who had a loved one in prison, people she had plenty of time to get to know as they endured the lengthy process of just getting into the visitation room together.

"My politicization very much grew out of that commitment to the person next to me in line," Isa said. "I think it's really important that the work that we're doing is not just theoretical, but it also has an accountability that's grounded in people that you meet and the understanding that our liberation is connected."

Isa, who joined Critical Resistance in the summer of 2020 as an intern, is petite in stature, sports a buzz cut, and has a face that made her seem much younger than I assumed she was based on her recollections from childhood. On the day of our interview, she was wearing drawstring slacks with a white t-shirt and a gold chain. She took a moment to measure her response to each one of my questions, speaking articulately and with poise. As she dove deeper into the layers of the work that motivates her, however, her speech became rapid, seemingly driven by equal parts nervousness, frustration, and passion.

For example, I mentioned a recent *New York Times* article that had profiled Susanville locals who feared their lives would be upended should either or both of the local prisons close,[4] but Isa quickly and poignantly countered with an explanation that exemplifies how the coalition is working to change that narrative.

"I think a lot of times the argument is made that if you were to remove a prison from a prison town, that local economy would be destroyed. But when you look at the actual numbers of it, for Susanville, 18 percent of the people living in that town are living below the poverty line with a per capita income of $13,800. And so we can clearly see that having a prison did *not* support the local economy. Susanville's a town that has not just one but two California state prisons:

CCC [California Correctional Center] and High Desert State Prison. So the prison system has this economic chokehold on the town where nothing else can be built—no schools, no colleges, no other types of tourism—because there's a prison in that town, so no one wants to go into that town or build or invest."

Isa gasped for air.

"Plus, if a town's economic survivability is dependent on systemic racism and institutions that emotionally, physically, and psychologically harm other human beings in cages, then we need to rethink our economics."

At the end of her explanation, she wrung her hands together, and Viju brought her back to center with a calm, "That was really good."

She breathed, finally.

"Oh God, I'm dying out here," she said with a slight rouge tinting her freckled cheeks. I was reminded that most organizers in this space have the experience of being one in a crowd, one in a community, not the one behind the microphone.

The OG

Many abolitionists talk about the moment they were "radicalized." Maybe it was the first time they saw the inhumane nature of prison after visiting an incarcerated loved one, like Isa. Maybe the viral videos of unarmed Black men being gunned down by police officers started the ball rolling. Angela Davis has said she believes she was born radicalized.

Born in Birmingham, Alabama, in 1944, Angela told attendees of a 2021 symposium that she "came out of the womb demanding change." Her mother was active in the Southern Negro Youth Congress, an organization founded by the children of National Negro Congress members with the mission of defending the civil rights of Black people in the South. Angela's childhood included neighborhood bombings by the Ku Klux Klan. Black fathers in her community worked as miners and steelworkers, jobs they had inherited from Black convicts forced to do such work under the leasing system of the late nineteenth century. The Birmingham Angela grew up in was the most segregated city in the country, and her mother raised the children to view this as abnormal, rather than allow them to find comfort in the status quo.

"She had this profound impact on us," Angela said at the symposium. "She demanded we imagine a different world."[5]

The first time I met Angela was at the inauguration of former San Francisco DA Chesa Boudin. She was easy to pick out of the crowd. She stood above most of the attendees at five-foot-eight—almost six feet in her heels. Under the house lights of the Herbst Theatre, her iconic silhouette, her Afro now a brilliant blend of white and gray, emanated an ethereal glow that highlighted the soft features of her face. Her eyes, behind thin, frameless glasses, showed the weariness of years of struggle yet the ferocity for a fight that still lay ahead. Her brow naturally furrowed when conversing, and she spoke with a low, drawn-out cadence. Angela conquered the dramatic pause long before Barack Obama made it cool.

Our paths began to cross more often after that, as I left the DA's office to join All of Us or None, one of many grassroots organizations that emerged from a conference Critical Resistance hosted in 1998.

Over 3,500 activists attended that event, billed as "Beyond the Prison Industrial Complex: A National Conference and Strategy Session." The event attracted academics, former prisoners, labor leaders, religious organizations, feminists, LGBTQ activists, and policymakers from every US state and several foreign countries. Over three days, these attendees participated in 200 different panels and workshops and were treated to several cultural events, including a film festival.[6]

The gathering led to anti-carceral individuals and organizations forming a foundational coalition. Together, the coalition launched a counteroffensive to California's "build them and fill them" era between 1977 and 2007, defined by the development of twenty prisons and a prison population that increased by 900 percent, from 19,623 to 174,282.[7] The movement spurred by the 1998 conference would celebrate many progressive victories in the following decades, including the passages of significant, decarceration-focused ballot measures, such as Proposition 47, which recategorized some nonviolent felony offenses as misdemeanors, and Prop 57, which allowed parole consideration for nonviolent felons and authorized sentence credits for good behavior and participation in educational programs. To date, these propositions, along with similar reforms, contributed to a 30 percent reduction in the prison population over the course of a decade (2006–2017) and an incarceration rate—the number of adults incarcerated by the state for every 100,000 residents—lower than any year since the 1980s.[8]

Through this work, Critical Resistance has fine-tuned its three-prong strategy for campaigns: grassroots outreach, legislative advocacy, and media campaigns. In fighting on all three fronts simultaneously, organizers have been able to accomplish several first-of-their-kind victories.

Its first big win was against then-city attorney John Russo's gang injunctions. In 2010 Russo sought to combat crime in Oakland by flooding certain areas with uniformed officers—a tactic known as *hotspot policing*—and designated the neighborhoods of North Oakland and Fruitvale to be not only hotspots but "gang zones." Individuals who encountered law enforcement in these designated zones would be subjected to arrest for minor violations, like breaking curfew, as well as sentence enhancements and longer stays in prison.

"Anti-gang civil injunctions promise to perpetuate racial stigma and oppression," writes Gary Stewart in the *Yale Law Journal*. "Although justified in less overtly racist terms, anti-gang injunctions share with postbellum vagrancy ordinances a repressive effect that stamps minority communities with badges of inferiority."[9]

Stewart found that gang injunctions are no more than police-induced gentrification dressed up as crime fighting. Data at the time of Russo's injunctions would seem to validate this theory: In 2010, Oakland police records indicate that 72 percent of Oakland's homicides occurred in West Oakland's District 3 and East Oakland's Districts 6 and 7—all outside the area covered by the two injunctions.

North Oakland and Fruitvale do, however, border a trendy shopping district called Temescal. Peppered with boutique shops, microbreweries, and fine dining, Temescal had quickly gone from one of Oakland's oldest neighborhoods to one of its trendiest, rendering it ripe for an influx of wealthy and white newcomers. Within a year of Russo's gang injunction initiation, the Black population of Oakland had decreased by 25 percent, with North Oakland being the most impacted neighborhood.[10] An Oakland police officer at the time likened the department's enforcement of injunctions to an "invading army."[11]

While the American Civil Liberties Union took Russo to court—and lost—Critical Resistance formed a coalition of community organizations to deploy its three-prong strategy. The Stop the Injunctions Coalition (STIC) hosted political education events in schools and community spaces to open a dialogue about policing, safety, and gentrification. Attendees received talking points, fact sheets, and a Know Your Rights pocket guide. The media team trained individuals who had been impacted by the injunctions to serve as spokespeople and filled city council meetings with hundreds of constituents.

"We just have unfortunate skin color, and I hate to say it that way because I have pride in who I am," said Jessica Hollie, a grassroots activist, at a 2013 Oakland City Council meeting.[12]

That meeting, which lasted nine hours, ultimately did not go the coalition's way; the council approved the hiring of police chief Bill Bratton, who supported the injunctions. But Critical Resistance kept up the pressure: In addition to returning to City Hall several times, organizers held a block party where they filmed testimonies of neighborhood residents impacted by the injunctions. The STIC grassroots and media outreach teams proliferated those videos on social channels and sent clips directly to several media outlets.

Finally, in 2015, STIC became the first grassroots campaign in history to defeat gang injunctions. The city not only ended the injunctions in Fruitvale and North Oakland but committed to not pursue future injunctions.

"Our work together inspired people targeted by the injunctions to become powerful organizers," read a coalition statement announcing its victory. "It unified Black and Brown communities across the entire city in a common struggle, and drew us together to forge stronger bonds."[13]

For the first decade of its existence, Critical Resistance mainly focused on bringing together various abolitionist organizers for strategy sessions. It hosted numerous conferences after its successful 1998 gathering, each one growing in attendance and solidifying relationships with similarly missioned organizations. The coalition to Close California Prisons is largely a result of longtime relationships that began during those years. The victory against gang injunctions took Critical Resistance into a new evolution of campaign work as it entered its second decade.

"When I arrived in 2010, we were relatively new in practicing a few things and our campaign against gang injunctions solidified our three-pronged strategy as a way of winning an abolitionist campaign," CR's Woods Ervin said. "Legislative, grassroots, and media outreach became the pistons that drove the work forward."

Personal Revolution

Woods, who identifies as nonbinary and uses they/them pronouns, grew up a Black, queer kid in the South, which meant their familiarity with law enforcement came early and often. They remember cousins and classmates "disappearing" for significant lengths of time, their female relatives troubleshooting how to maintain a semi-normal family life with the family constantly in flux.

Woods describes their radicalization as simply the logical outcome for someone growing up during the early 2000s. In the summer of 2005, they watched what they term the "rapid dispossession and gentrification" of poor Black communities in New Orleans following Hurricane Katrina, as the federal government's revitalization plans and relief efforts deprioritized or omitted Black-majority areas like the

Lower Ninth Ward. A year later, Chicago, where Woods had relocated to attend Northwestern, joined the national boycott known as a Day Without an Immigrant, also called the Great American Boycott. The boycott, which took place in nearly every major US city thanks to the proliferation of the idea on social media, intended to demonstrate the important role immigrants played in the economy—by having thousands of them in the streets rather than at work—and, in Chicago, galvanized crowds as large as 400,000 people, including Woods.[14]

Around the same time, Woods underwent a personal revolution as they began to identify as a nonbinary trans person. They began to seek out other Black trans youth in Chicago, many of whom were homeless and heavily policed.

"I was seeing Black and poor people in the South being dispossessed by the federal government, thinking about that dispossession on an international scale, and trying to support young people who are just like me and having them constantly be imprisoned because they couldn't be folded into the mainstream," Woods said. "These things starkly led me into an understanding of the relationship between the economy, policing, imprisonment, and poor people."

Woods joined Critical Resistance in 2010 to assist in the campaign to end gang injunctions. They remained active in the Oakland chapter, doing research and outreach for subsequent campaigns like No New SF Jails, which successfully defeated plans to build a new jail in 2015 and forced the closure of County Jail 4 in 2020. That year, CR hired Woods as the director of programs, a position that has made them a media spokesperson for several campaigns including Close California Prisons.

Somewhere in all that, Woods found time to collaborate with some of the most established leaders of the abolitionist movement today: From 2014 to 2018 they helped rebuild Miss Major Griffin-Gracy's Transgender Gender Variant Intersex Justice Project, and recently became a research assistant at Interrupting Criminalization, a data-driven abolitionist think tank led by Mariame Kaba and Andrea J. Ritchie.

It sounds exhausting, but Woods has found ways to maintain sanity and stamina. Like many people I've met in this space, Woods has a sense of humor and finds ways to laugh at some of the more frustrating elements of progressive movements, elements emanating from both within and outside leftist circles. Woods sets off humor bombs in the face of misinformed—and usually offensive, or racist, or a combination of the two—opponents of decriminalization, and establishment politicians who claim to be leftist but hedge and balk as they reach for more moderate voters.

Woods laughs with their whole body, starting with the deepening of their dimples and ending with a bowl over, their eyes squinting behind black-rimmed glasses that nearly take a tumble as their head rebounds back into place. Their words begin to elevate to a higher octave than their more poised responses, and their Southern roots begin to breach the surface in the form of the occasional "y'all."

In one of our conversations, I asked Woods about their personal collaborations, including the work they did with Interrupting Criminalization. The group had just released a report highlighting some of the major flaws in how law enforcement handles sexual assault. The report was entitled *What about the Rapists?*, a title I pause to give necessary deference to when I mention it to Woods.[15] They begin to rear back with closed eyes and pursed lips. They're trying not to break.

I push a little: "I mean, I think I've been asked this question by literally every member of the California legislature at this point . . ."

"It's like they're robots!" They break. They're howling laughing and now so am I. "I look at them and I'm like, 'How do y'all have the same question?!'"

From an abolitionist standpoint, the idea that sexual assault victims somehow get justice from the current system is almost laughable. According to a 2015 National Domestic Violence Hotline survey, 80 percent of sexual assault survivors are afraid to call the police, 30 percent felt less safe after calling the police, and 24 percent of survivors who called the police were arrested or threatened with arrest. Only 5 percent of the rapes that were reported to the police led to the perpetrator being arrested and even fewer—3 percent—led to a conviction. Seventy percent choose not to report their sexual assault to authorities at all.[16]

"As police and prison abolitionists, we're saying that the 70 percent of people who are already outside of the system deserve more and better options," the cleverly named report states. "For many survivors, relying on police to keep us safe from rapists is like fighting fire with gasoline."

Woods continues with their near-delirious reaction to the absurdity that searching for an alternative to the current system is somehow less justice for victims.

"What are *y'all* doing about the rapists?" they say. "Like that should be *our* question: What *about* them?!"

Shutdowns

After I met with CR's Isa and Viju, I was invited to sit in on a virtual meeting the coalition was having to see how the engine gears up in real time. Some weeks later, I signed on to the video conferencing application as a diverse group of individuals began to populate the mosaic interface. After some casual chatter about note-taking and scheduling conflicts as well as a brief introduction about my presence and intent, the meeting got underway with the moderator screen-sharing a document outlining the agenda. The main focus of this particular meeting would be decision-makers. Elizabeth from Show Up for Racial Justice (SURJ) reported back on a recent call she had with Natasha Minsker, a strategic consultant who had access to the governor's office.

"She said the three biggest barriers to Newsom taking more action [on closing prisons] were the California Correctional Peace Officers Association [and its associated union], legislators representing towns where prisons are being closed, and the threat of possible future disasters like pandemics and wildfires," Elizabeth said. "Her note says, 'Newsom is also sensitive about what we saw with the pandemic—unexpected events happen, and if you have fewer prisons open you have less flexibility to move folks around in the event of an emergency.'"

A brief pause followed Elizabeth's presentation to allow for everyone's eyeballs to finish their circles. Of course, for abolitionists, the idea of people burning alive in a cage from wildfires—something that nearly happened in Susanville that very summer—or being trapped in a superspreader of a deadly virus is a humanitarian crisis and a good reason to close prisons, not keep them open.

The meeting continued with a power-mapping activity, where coalition members identified allies, neutrals, opponents, and their respective levels of power and influence. For example, the California Correctional Peace Officers Association (CCPOA) holds a tremendous amount of power both in numbers (approximately 30,000 dues-paying individuals) and influence: In 2016, for example, the association established a PAC with $8.2 million in member contributions.[17] To combat this, the coalition needs to identify equally powerful allies. They do so by placing Jennifer Kim and Chris Francis, two of the governor's budget consultants, on the equal but opposite side of the map as the CCPOA. Kim, who serves on the legislature's public safety committee, has been outspoken about the need to reform the state's juvenile detention policies, and Francis was the lead budget advisor for criminal justice reform and judiciary issues between 2018 and 2021. While neither of them has the financial backing of the CCPOA, they certainly hold the keys to an even larger sum: the state's $306.5 billion in total state funds.[18]

Having identified the individuals and groups who are most likely to influence the governor's decisions on prison closure, the coalition started to refine the three prongs of its campaign: The legislative outreach team opts to set up meetings with Kim and Francis and to apply pressure to the Senate's Subcommittee on Corrections, Public Safety, Judiciary, Labor and Transportation by attending and speaking out at regular hearings. The media outreach team, noting the governor's "unexpected events" apprehension, decided to put together a plan to flip the narrative about public safety—to uplift the stories of incarcerated individuals who were, for example, threatened by the pandemic or nearby wildfires. The grassroots team agreed to design a campaign to collect stories from people in prison as well as their loved ones. They also pledged to mobilize public comment for both local events and the subcommittee hearings.

As its *dismantle* theory becomes reality, Critical Resistance works with its coalition partners on *change* and *build*. The majority of the facilities they propose prioritizing for closure are in California's Central Valley, towns populated by individuals as politically conservative as the Bay Area is politically liberal. Since CR's California chapters are located in the more progressive cities of Los Angeles and Oakland, its staff collaborates with organizations that have daily contact with locals in the state's central region. These local partners serve as conduits between the needs of the community and decisions being made by the coalition. In town hall settings, they will listen to residents' concerns and promote community-oriented avenues of investment— using the cost of imprisonment to develop mental health services, increase wages for local workers, ameliorate education systems, and so on. This "common-sense resource allocation," as organizers term it, rethinks public safety by focusing on community needs rather than punitive retaliation.

"We're building power in coalitions, in our campaigns, to get material wins by taking power away from the PIC and putting that self-determination and agency back into the community," Viju said. "We're part of different local grassroots efforts to figure out what the needs of the community are, how we can help, and how we can plug in to make prison closure in that place a reality."

Abolition by Default

You've read a little about the prison-industrial complex in chapter 2 and how all prisons have some form of penal labor, but the presence of a widescale profiting mechanism within the California prison system is especially acute. There are 70 factories in California's 33 prisons.

Between 2014 and 2015, these facilities earned $207 million in revenue, or $58 million in profit from the labor of incarcerated workers, either by offsetting costs for prison maintenance, selling prison-manufactured goods, or contracting with private companies.[19] Some 7,000 incarcerated workers are overseen by the California Prison Industry Authority, a state agency, which uses prison labor to manufacture everything from US flags, license plates, and packaged candy to office furniture for various state buildings and schools.[20]

These "jobs" are not voluntary. Curtis Howard, a founding member of All of Us or None San Diego, said he rebelled against work assignments, haunted by his "ancestral lineage," and was penalized with time added to his already lengthy sentence. The labor cannot even qualify as rehabilitation or reentry efforts because many equivalent positions on the outside require state licenses—licenses the state denies to individuals with conviction histories.

"In California alone, [economists Morris Kleiner and Evgeny Vorotnikov] estimate that licensure has eliminated almost 196,000 jobs, has resulted in $840.4 million in lost annual output, and has created a $22.1 billion annual misallocation of resources," Matthew Mitchell, an economist and senior research fellow at the Mercatus Center at George Mason University, told the California Senate Standing Committee on Business, Professions, and Economic Development in 2019. "By their estimates, California's licensing regime is costlier than that of any other state in the nation."[21]

Unsurprisingly, the Prison Industry Authority's biggest customer is the prison system itself, accounting for about two-thirds of sales. All the furniture in Ivan Kilgore's cell, for example, is stamped with "PIA." And while the PIA does partner with the private sector (see p. 24), the majority of the prison "workforce"—about 95 percent—hold prison maintenance jobs, such as laundry, food prep, and janitorial duties. In buying materials produced by the cheap labor it forces upon its population, and by creating workforces around maintenance, the prison department offsets the majority of its operating costs, allowing administrators and staff to line their pockets with the remainder.

Consequently, prison guards in California receive a higher base salary than their counterparts in any other jurisdiction, including the Federal Bureau of Prisons.

"Because of the extent to which prison building and operation began to attract vast amounts of capital—from the construction industry to food and health care provision—in a way that recalled the emergence of the military industrial complex, we began to refer to a 'prison industrial complex,'" Angela Davis wrote in her 2003 book *Are Prisons Obsolete?*.[22]

For most of the twenty-first century, progressive politics has erred on the side of reform when it comes to combating the prison-industrial complex. Electronic monitoring, for example, was considered a preferable alternative to incarceration. Instead, electronic monitoring, like the anklet that bankrupted Ali, has allowed law enforcement to extend imprisonment beyond prisons and jails. The devices also serve to generate further profits for the prison-industrial complex, with large-scale use of monitors like "the Guardian" being sold by ViaPath Technologies (formerly Global Tel Link, or GTL), the sole provider of phone services to prisons and jails in the state. In this way, rather than curbing the continued growth of American incarceration, reform has allowed it to evolve; the prison-industrial complex continues to scale up and turn profits far beyond prison walls.

CR makes an argument for abolition by default, highlighting the fact that prisons were originally established as a more humane punishment than death. Not only do we continue to perform state-sponsored executions, a method even Jonas Hanway and his contemporaries three centuries ago considered to be archaic, but innovations such as indefinite solitary confinement and twenty-three-hour lockdowns have served to make the system more expansive and more oppressive.

"What was once regarded as progressive and even revolutionary represents today the marriage of technological superiority and political backwardness," Angela Davis writes. "No one—not even the most ardent defenders of the supermax—would try to argue today that absolute segregation, including sensory deprivation, is restorative and healing."[23]

Critical Resistance's founders have looked at the various evolutions and reforms of the prison system, including the rise of the prison-industrial complex, and have implemented organizing techniques that fight the beast without setting off a rash of snakeheads. Part of the political education that new organizers receive, for example, is a word of caution about carve-outs—caveats that preclude prisoners of certain offenses from various legislative reforms—and exception clauses. After all, it is the exception clause in the 13th Amendment that allows the prison-industrial complex to generate profits off slave labor. This means moving away from propositions that focus on "non-violent offenders" and toward more-inclusive demands.

"We're not going to divide who we're calling for freedom for," Isa explained. "We know that when you only call for the freedom of people with certain types of offenses, you're actually building a brick wall that makes it that much harder for us to be able to dismantle when we go back for the rest of our folks."

Stuff in the Margins

In *Defund Fear*, Zach Norris uses his own experience of having his home broken into to examine alternatives to punishment and possible alternatives to crime prevention. At the beginning of the book, he unpacks the moment he came home to find the windows of his daughters' room shattered.

"The true threat in this story was not the would-be burglary, but the stuff in the margins—a fragmented healthcare system with a racial bias, the radical wealth inequality that causes widespread poverty. Both are the calculated outcomes of a system that prioritizes profit over humanity, for the benefit of a powerful few."[24]

Organizers do not think of abolition as a destructive practice. Rather, prison dismantlement is a means to opening up space—both physical space and in states' budgets—to build something new.

Instead of prioritizing profits over humanity, it reallocates prison-industrial profits into those "stuff in the margins."

"Even with the warm shutdown [of Deuel Vocational Institution], there's a savings of $110,000," Viju explained. "That's $110,000 for public schools in Tracy."

At the time of this writing, California is on the brink of closing its second prison, the California Correctional Center in Susanville, which was profiled by the *New York Times*. A February 2023 report from the Legislative Analyst's Office said the state can close up to nine additional prisons while still complying with a federal court order that dictates each facility's maximum capacity.[25] With the three prisons already slated for closure, the coalition may exceed its goal, as twelve prisons are now identified for closure by the state's own analysis.

This analysis, of course, is based purely on numbers: The state prison population had dropped from its peak in 2006 of 165,000 to 95,000 in 2023. There are also budgetary numbers: The state's operating cost for its prisons is $18 billion annually.[26]

"Difficult decisions have to be made," said Caitlin O'Neil, one of the report's authors. "But if we don't make those decisions, the alternative is paying hundreds of millions for prison beds we don't need to be paying for."[27]

This viewpoint is, of course, strategically sound: If anything can sway more conservative members of the state legislature—and the general public, for that matter—it would be fiscal responsibility. But there's a more community-based element that can appeal to voters.

"The way we get [to abolition] is by changing the narrative and changing people's understanding of what we need to keep us safe," said Viju. "We don't actually need more cops or more prisons in the community. What we need is housing, healthcare, education, and things like that. As we shift away from the PIC, we're putting those funds or those resources toward those institutions."

In September 2022, Lassen County Judge Robert F. Moody ruled against a preliminary injunction to stall shutdown efforts in Susanville, citing the fiscal imprudence of the state's prison maintenance.[28]

A few months later, the corrections department announced it would not renew its lease with CoreCivic for California City Correctional Facility, terminating the contract in March 2024 and adding a fourth facility to its list of confirmed closures.[29] In Tracy the warm shutdown provoked CURB to draw up a Prison Closure Roadmap. Published in February 2023, it details how the state can safely shut down prisons completely, without repurposing them or having them continue to drain resources.[30]

With town halls and community meetings underway in prison towns across the state, the opportunities for what comes next are vast. And while there is an urge to demand an immediate solution, abolitionists such as Mariame Kaba believe the urge to at least imagine beyond incarceration is far greater.

"When you say, 'What would we do without prisons?' what you are really saying is: 'What would we do without civil death, exploitation, and state-sanctioned violence?'" Kaba said in her bestselling book *We Do This 'Til We Free Us: Abolitionist Organizing and Transforming Justice.* "That is an old question and the answer remains the same: whatever it takes to build a society that does not continuously rearrange the trappings of annihilation and bondage while calling itself 'free.'"[31]

Bigger than Life by Scotty Scott aka Scott W. Smith

Reimagining Capitalism:
Greenwood

On a brisk December morning in 2022, Democratic Senate candidate Raphael G. Warnock walked into the SWAG Shop, a barbershop in Atlanta's west side. He casually sat down on one of the red, cushioned chairs and sank in.

Warnock was not at the SWAG Shop for a shave or a cut. He was there to make one final appeal to voters who would be heading to the polls the following day for the Georgia Senate runoff election. Seated beside him was the shop's owner, Mike Render, a rapper better known as Killer Mike.

"The barbershop is . . . a social center, especially in African American communities, where you find out who did what," Mike told the crowd of constituents and media personnel. "I've been terribly impressed by this man as a human being, as a member of the clergy, and as a politician. I am here today to give a shot to him so that we may all give an ear to him. We should get out to the polls."[1]

The fact that Warnock's final day of campaigning began at the SWAG Shop speaks to Killer Mike's influence on the culture beyond his artistic endeavors. Known primarily for his role in the rap duo Run the Jewels, Mike has used his success in the music business to fund several enterprises in Atlanta. He opened the SWAG Shop in 2011 with his wife, Shana, adorning it with black, red, and yellow decor. The storefront illuminates the sidewalk on Edgewood Avenue, with an all-red finish, black tinted windows, and a yellow stamp logo featuring the shop's name. A black shingle hangs above the entrance with *The SWAG Shop* written in yellow type. On a day when the shop is filled with patrons, not politicians, the soft hum of electric trimmers radiates from the cushioned chairs. Black floors. Yellow letters. Red chairs.

The color scheme has become something of a trademark of Mike's various businesses. In 2018 he bought Bankhead Seafood, a fifty-five-year-old restaurant he had frequented as a child, with rapper T. I. and developer Noel Khalil.[2] While the brick-and-mortar restaurant is still under redevelopment, a Bankhead food truck draws in crowds. Block yellow letters spelling out *Bankhead Seafood* encircle a silhouette of a red, scaly fish standing in stark contrast to the all-black truck body. Black truck. Yellow letters. Red fish.

The colors suit him: Black and red are staples of the city he adores, with three professional sports teams—the Falcons (NFL), Atlanta United (MLS), and the Hawks (NBA)—all represented by black and red logos. But they are also "power colors," demanding attention, as Mike himself often does when it comes to the issues impacting his community locally as a Black man in Atlanta and nationally as a Black man in America.

"I don't give a shit about liking you or you liking me," he told *GQ* magazine in the summer of 2020. "What I give a shit about is if your policies are going to benefit me and my community in a way that will help us get a leg up in America."[3]

Atlanta is a city bursting with color, with street art serving as a trademark of the city walls. Not too far from the SWAG Shop is the heavily trafficked tapestry of the Beltline, the city's main railway. The dim lighting of lamp posts creates an angelic hue around the depiction of a young girl in a blue dress imprinted on the walls. The child, a representation of Carrie Steele, who founded the city's first orphanage for children of color, stands among waves of orange and blue, peppered with small, black symbols that look like miniature parachutes. Nearby a neon-green frog seemingly pops out of the wall, with wide, fiery eyes and reddish-orange webbing. Aquamarine silhouettes and yellow graffiti tags add to the cacophony of color emanating from the cavernous underbelly of the mass transit system. Red storefronts. Neon frogs. Orange waves.

But, according to the local #BankBlack movement, one color trumps them all: Green.

A Rapper, an Entrepreneur, and a Civil Rights Hero Walk into a Bank

Killer Mike's theory of change has become something of a mantra, promoted in the many public appearances he makes and custom merch he proudly adorns. According to Mike, activism requires five main components: plotting, planning, strategizing, organizing, and mobilizing. Here's the Cliffs Notes version:

Plot: come up with an idea

Plan: put that idea down on paper

Strategize: take that paper and come up with an action plan

Organize: get input on that plan from others and encourage them to join you

Mobilize: deploy the plan of action by engaging the larger community

Greenwood, the digital bank Mike cofounded as a type of financial protest, shows how strict adherence to this rather simple design for change can create a large-scale impact.

It began in 2016, before Mike admittedly knew what a fintech—financial technology—company was. That year MTV News and BET News hosted a town hall to discuss "America in Crisis," which took place at the end of a tumultuous week: Police had killed three Black men—Delrawn Small, Alton Sterling, and Philando Castile—and videos of their brutal deaths were dominating newscasts and social media channels. With protests raging across the country, a weary but impassioned Mike called into the town hall to **plot** a new kind of resistance.[4]

"We know that this country is motivated by two very real things— violence and money—and we cannot go out in the street to engage in acts of violence that will cause more peril to our community and to people who look like us," he relayed to Charlamagne tha God, one of the town hall moderators and a personal friend. "I encourage us to take our warfare to financial institutions."

Mike then proceeded to lay out a definitive **plan:** He encouraged one million people to find one Black banking institution, like Citizens Trust, and open a $100 account "instead of buying Jordans or caps or whatever thing is cool this month." Assuming the full million took action, Black banks would have a lending power of $100 million and the ability to offer Black families home loans in areas being gentrified. These banks also could make small business loans of $15,000 to $18,000, the kind of loans traditional banks wouldn't float Mike himself for his first business venture.

The #BankBlack hashtag proliferated Mike's theory for change over the weekend, and by the following week, Citizens Trust reported 8,000 new accounts.[5] Tellers reported people "swarming" the bank's Atlanta branches.[6] For so long, Black-owned banks, which typically had been operating with a lending power in the hundreds of thousands, had been woefully behind mainstream banks like Wells Fargo or Bank of America operating in the trillions. But Mike's call spoke to people, and a BankBlack coalition was formed from young people dedicated to seeing the mission through. They mobilized communities nationwide, and within a year, most Black-owned banks—at that time there were only twenty-three nationwide—were reporting surges in new accounts; bank assets grew by roughly $60 million.[7]

In addition to everyday citizens, Black celebrities and business owners began to take action. By the summer of 2016, serial entrepreneur Ryan Glover was in his fifth year at the helm of Bounce TV, a television station he founded to be "the first 24/7 digital multi-cast broadcast network created to target African Americans."[8] Killer Mike's message piqued his interest.

"Many entrepreneurs like myself, because of our historically shaky banking relationships with traditional financial institutions or lenders, don't even think about going to banks to borrow money for capital," Ryan said. "My grandmother, you know, her savings and depository institution was her mattress."

African American communities have valid reasons not to trust the American banking system. Centuries of redlining—the practice of denying home and business loans to consumers from neighbor-hoods with significant numbers of racial and ethnic minorities and low-income residents—paralyzed generational wealth building and exacerbated the so-called wealth gap between white Americans and their Black counterparts.

"Equity that families have in their homes is the main source of wealth for middle-class Americans," Richard Rothstein writes. "Afri-can American families today, whose parents and grandparents were denied participation in the equity-accumulating boom of the 1950s and 1960s, have great difficulty catching up now."[9]

"We've not experienced a hundred years of freedom," Killer Mike told me. "My parents were born in apartheid. They call it 'Jim Crow'—that sounds cute—but it wasn't. It was apartheid. It was a system that did not allow us to take full advantage of the American dream, which is built on the blood and toil of us, out of the cotton fields and out of the industrial revolution that came as a result of cotton picking."

Through entrepreneurship, Ryan had been successful at alle-viating financial burdens for his own family, but he began thinking about ways to make a larger impact on his community. A year after Mike's call-in to MTV, Ryan sold Bounce to E. W. Scripps Com-pany and promptly made two phone calls: one to the former mayor of Atlanta and United Nations ambassador Andrew Young, who had been part of the original ownership team at Bounce TV; and one to

Killer Mike. He wanted his next venture to be a fintech company, and he wanted Andrew and Mike to be cofounders. A businessman, an activist/politician, and a rapper: The trifecta embodies the power and potential of the Black community in the city they call home.

"Mike and Ambassador Young and I come from quasi-different professional backgrounds, but our messages to our community have always been the same," said Ryan. "We are about the advancement of Black and Brown people through having access to capital."

Like other fintech companies—Chime, Aspiration, and Varo, to name a few—their company, Greenwood, proposed a completely digital offering of checking and savings accounts with mobile deposits and peer-to-peer transfer capabilities. A sleek platinum black card provides holders access to a global ATM network and mobile wallet services.

What differentiates Greenwood is its mission-driven **strategy** to finance Black and Latino clientele. Its banking services are provided through its partnership with Coastal Community Bank, allowing its founders and members of the board to focus on community empowerment and growing generational wealth among Black and Latino families. Customers can opt to round up expenditures to the nearest dollar and donate the change to charities like the King Center for Nonviolent Social Change, the National Association for the Advancement of Colored People, and the United Negro College Fund. The company uses relationships with FDIC-insured banks to fund a monthly $10,000 grant to a Black or Latino small business owner who has an account with Greenwood. It has committed to providing five free meals to an in-need family for every customer sign-up through its partnership with Goodr, a local organization that uses blockchain technology to repurpose edible surplus food.[10]

"Our mission is to create non-predatory lending products, to help recirculate capital within our community, and to deploy capital to deserving borrowers, whether it is for personal or business use," Ryan said. "Ambassador Young would always joke and say, 'We didn't have sit-ins at Walgreens to have a ham sandwich at the counter. We wanted to be able to buy the Walgreens.'"

The founders began to **organize** the offerings and programs that would make Greenwood both a successful fintech company and a successful economic protest. In 2020 the company circulated its idea to the private sector. The campaign raised $3 million in seed funding and $40 million of Series A funding from six of the seven largest US banks and the top two payment technology companies: Truist, Bank of America, PNC, JPMorgan Chase, Wells Fargo, Mastercard, and Visa.[11] Naturally, I wondered how partnering with some of the worst offenders of redlining impacted the integrity of the initiative.

"I believe it takes collaboration and community, a village if you will, to extinguish the multigenerational wealth gap that exists in America," Ryan offered. "I can't look at what happened 100 years ago, because my job now is to look forward: to help people like me, who look like me, who have the same hunger, drive, and determination that I have, to reach their goals and dreams in America. So that's what I'm laser-focused on: looking forward, not behind."

Buoyed by the momentum of #BankBlack, the credibility of its founders, and its successful funding campaigns, BankGreenwood.com launched in January 2022. Within a week, the waitlist for opening an account was 100,000 deep.

At the heart of Greenwood's efforts to **mobilize** its customers is financial literacy. Shortly after opening the waitlist, the bank launched Greenwood Studios, a collection of multimedia resources to inform customers on how best to use or invest their earnings. It produces a daily podcast, *Money Moves*, hosted by tech maven and *Real Housewives of Atlanta* personality Tanya Sam, who invites expert guests to discuss financial planning tips. Greenwood financial planner Rianka R. Dorsainvil has a series of video tutorials on handling personal finance decisions, from building generational wealth to making sound investments. Poised Lifestyle founder Sahirenys Pierce partnered with Greenwood to offer a biweekly Q&A called "Ask Me Anything about Money," where Pierce answers queries sent in via social media.[12]

The company also offers an online database of Black- and Latino-owned businesses across the country. The Greenbook lets site visitors enter their geographic location, then populates a list of qualifying businesses, sortable by industry.

"Time and time again, Blacks have figured out how to individually liberate themselves—whether it be Herman Russell, Madam C. J. Walker, or Oprah Winfrey," Mike said. "That's not the same as creating a culture where you grow culturally competent children who can then participate in the greater society and have an opportunity to have something for themselves."

Black Wall Street

Some critics argue that capitalism and abolition are fundamentally at odds. They point out that historical instances of human exploitation have often been driven by economic interests and profit motives. In this view, capitalism can perpetuate the exploitative practices that abolition seeks to eliminate. In a 2020 interview with *Democracy Now!*, for example, Angela Davis said, "I am convinced that the ultimate eradication of racism is going to require us to move toward a more socialist organization of our economies."[13] Abolitionists of this ilk point to slavery, convict leasing, and prison labor as proof that capitalism will inevitably give rise to dehumanization and manipulation.

The relationship between abolition and capitalism can vary depending on how each is conceptualized and implemented within a society. Greenwood's founders believe an intersectional approach is possible, that economic growth and prosperity can provide alternatives to forced labor, making such practices less appealing. Additionally, in advocating for Black- and Latino-owned businesses that prioritize ethical practices, fair treatment of workers, and a commitment to uplift members of the Black and Latino communities, Greenwood's reimagined capitalism purports to address not only economic inequality but racial inequalities as well.

The guiding force behind this belief is embodied in the name *Greenwood*. In the early 1900s, the Greenwood district of Tulsa, Oklahoma, was known as Black Wall Street, a place thriving with Black-owned businesses and intra-community currency exchange. While research on racial wealth gaps suggests that less than 3 percent of the Black communities' $1 trillion in buying power is reinvested into community businesses, historians believe every dollar in Greenwood would exchange hands nineteen times before it entered the mainstream (read: white) economy.[14]

Founded by wealthy Black landowner O. W. Gurley, the town of Greenwood was a fully self-contained epicenter for former slaves fleeing racism and oppression in the post–Civil War South. After purchasing the land, Gurley set up several boarding houses for African Americans who arrived with minimal resources. He then provided loans for Greenwood residents who wished to start a business. Over time, members of the community built restaurants, movie theaters, a library, clothing stores, grocery stores, barbershops and salons, and offices for doctors, lawyers, and dentists. Residents used the profits from these amenities to establish a Greenwood school system, newspaper, post office, savings and loan bank, hospital, and bus and taxi service.[15]

"It doesn't take money to get power," Killer Mike explained. "It takes organization, it takes the want to win, but once you get money, in my opinion, you are responsible to help others empower themselves."

Mike grew up in Collier Heights, a neighborhood with a similar foundation to Greenwood. It was financed, designed, and built by middle-class Black Atlantans for middle-class Black families. His neighbors included congressional representatives Cynthia and James McKinney, and developer Herman Russell, whose company's portfolio includes the Georgia Dome, Turner Field, and Hartsfield-Jackson Atlanta International Airport. The neighborhood was also home to the Shrine of the Black Madonna, a Pan African Orthodox church founded as a response to the specific theological, spiritual, and psychological needs of African Americans. Mike grew up with Atlanta's first Black mayor, Maynard Jackson—the first of six consecutive Black mayors—who withheld city funds from banks that refused to diversify their boards, forcing financial institutions to increase their inclusion of Black Americans. In very obvious ways, Collier Heights embodied the same kind of self-sufficiency that allowed Greenwood and Black communities to thrive.

At least for Mike, the takeaway lessons from communities like Greenwood and Collier Heights generate the foundational pillars of his financial revolution: circulate dollars intra-communally; reinvest profits into Black-owned businesses; and shift power by creating financial independence and generational wealth. Greenwood bank blends the historical success of the Greenwood district, the modern success of financial technology companies, and the momentum of the BankBlack movement to create a space where Black people are empowered by access to capital.

"I think that Black people need to see ourselves saving something for ourselves, because the stronger that we are as a community financially, the stronger the greater community becomes," Mike said. "When that community dollar is strong, it affects the bigger community in a stronger way, because they can participate in a fair way, and in a just way, versus just having dollars to give and never get anything in return."

Mike has always been "political," highly influenced by his grandmother's involvement with Dr. Martin Luther King Jr.'s Southern Christian Leadership Conference. But his radicalization came from the revolutionary organizers he grew up with in Collier Heights. Mike would meet Black Panthers and members of the Black Liberation Army and the Nation of Islam on his way to Frederick Douglass High School and learn about their philosophies.

"These are the people that were on the corners, encouraging us as young Black children to educate ourselves, to take care of ourselves," Mike told me. "What I started to see was, 'Oh, the things that my grandmother does, it has an even more radical side.' Like there are people who are like, 'Let's burn this shit down.'"

He credits two influential figures from his teenage years with the path he's been on as an activist and a changemaker for the last three decades: Alice Johnson, a community liaison for the Atlanta police department, and Edward Johnson (no relation), a teacher at the rival high school. Edward and Alice encouraged Mike and his peers to petition the city for a grant to hold a conference where they could articulate what they saw as the biggest problems facing the city at that time. Alice, who was on the mayor's youth council with Jean Childs Young, arranged for Mike and a few other students to meet with Jean's husband, then-mayor Andrew Young.

The mayor was intrigued: inner-city kids coming in and demanding funds to put on a conference, with an absolute prohibition of adult input. "We want to have a conference with young people, and let us decide for ourselves what we want to do," he remembers the students demanding. It was the kind of first impression that fosters long-term relationships and future partnerships. In this first partnership, Andrew gave Mike and his fellow organizers $500 and access to the Thomas B. Murphy Ballroom in the city's newly constructed World Congress Center.

On the Saturday of the event, the hall was filled with community members and public officials, all listening intently to the next generation of Atlantans articulating their ideas for a better future. And it wasn't what Andrew and other older Atlantans had anticipated in the social climate of the 1980s, when Black young people were perceived as getting caught up in drugs or gangs. Instead, these Atlanta teens cared about the quality of their education, health care, future employability, and global issues like world hunger.

"Adults thought kids cared about crime and getting beat up, but kids knew where to avoid going to get beat up and robbed," Mike remembered. "We cared about much more sophisticated, nuanced stuff than adults thought."

Mike caught the itch for organizing and never looked back.

"If I didn't have those people in my life to teach me to be an organizer, I would've been an aspirational organizer. I would've been a complainer. I might've popped up at a protest, but to be actively organizing means that on a daily, weekly, and monthly basis, you are about plotting, planning, strategizing, organizing, and mobilizing."

The conference had a lasting impact on the city's mayor as well. Andrew, who had been a close confidante of Dr. King, opted to attend a world hunger workshop at the conference. He distinctly remembers the leader, a kid who had just been released from jail, sharing an epiphany he had in lockup: He had seen Ethiopian children with their bellies distended and flies on their lips and thought, "Here I am complaining about the food they're giving us, but I'm getting three meals a day." Andrew then watched as the teen leaders developed a plan to collect donations by placing UNICEF cans on the countertops of local banks and stores. In the end, they donated roughly $100,000 to the famine in Ethiopia.

"I learned that where there's a will there's a way, and that young people can be very effective," Andrew told me.

The enthusiasm of Black youth is something Andrew sees as special to Atlanta. This is in large part because the city is home to five historically Black colleges and universities—Clark Atlanta University, where the first Black student legally challenged segregation in higher education in the Deep South; Morehouse College, the world's only HBCU for Black men; Morehouse School of Medicine, the first medical school established at an HBCU in the twentieth century; Spelman College, which boasts distinguished alumni such as Pulitzer Prize–winning author Alice Walker; and Morris Brown College, the first educational institution in Georgia to be owned and operated entirely by African Americans. Students from all these institutions were essential to the civil rights movement of the 1960s, regularly attending sit-ins and challenging exclusionary practices.

Andrew's involvement in Greenwood is very much a reverberation of that time. He had already earned his degree at Howard University when he moved to Atlanta in 1961. He was married and had spent the majority of his post-collegiate career as a pastor, befriending Dr. King along the way. He was working with the Southern Christian Leadership Conference to register Black voters when Fred Shuttlesworth, a minister from Birmingham, Alabama, came to visit.

"He came over and cussed us out," Andrew remembered. "He said there were sixty-some bombings in less than a year, and they weren't even getting in the paper in Atlanta. So we promised him we'd come over to Birmingham."

It was just before Christmas 1962, five months before the historic Birmingham campaign when 1,000 students would march down the main drag of one of the most racially divided cities in the country, when Dr. King approached Andrew.

"Andy, you know any white folks in Birmingham?" Andrew remembers him asking.

"I don't think I'd even spent a night in Birmingham," he told me, chuckling a bit at the memory. "But he said I had three months, and I told him I'd find some white folks to negotiate with and settle this."

Through connections from his pastoral days, Andrew reached out to members of the Episcopal diocese in Birmingham, eventually connecting with Bishop Coadjutor George M. Murray. Andrew pitched a meeting between Bishop Murray and Dr. King. Murray declined a face-to-face but agreed to pen a letter to open the lines of communication. "Letter from the Birmingham Jail," written after his arrest during the Birmingham demonstration, was Dr. King's response to Murray's initial correspondence.

"In spite of my shattered dreams, I came to Birmingham with the hope that the white religious leadership of this community would see the justice of our cause and, with deep moral concern, would serve as the channel through which our just grievances could reach the power structure," Dr. King wrote. "I had hoped that each of you would understand. But again I have been disappointed."[16]

It sounds very strategic and orchestrated. The Birmingham campaign and the correspondence between Dr. King and the clergy directly led to the 1964 Civil Rights Act. But Andrew sees it as a spiritual journey, the voyage of young men who simply put one foot in front of the other, not knowing where their steps would lead, and trusting the path had been paved by a higher being.

"[King] didn't know what he was writing," Andrew said about the letter. "He wrote most of it in the margins of a *New York Times* and finished it on toilet paper! He didn't know what it would lead to.

"There's an unknown in everything I've done," he continued. "It's the movement of the Spirit through the city of Atlanta."

Capitalism Ain't All That Bad

Andrew is more of a galvanizing figure for Greenwood than an active participant in its operations. The gravity of his presence on the board is profound, though, as he's lived a lifetime of milestones and achievements. Snapshots of these moments surround him in his crowded office at the Andrew Young Foundation, where he spoke to me over Zoom.

He was wearing a bright, Carolina-blue polo shirt, which stood in stark contrast to the dated photos that wallpapered the room. Above his furrowed brow and salt-and-pepper hair was a picture of the 1963 March on Washington, where Dr. King delivered his "I Have a Dream" speech. A separate portrait of the famous orator is close by, his chin resting on interlocked hands, eyes pointing in the direction of Andrew's chair as if listening to his responses to my questions.

Above Dr. King is a framed picture of Andrew with President Jimmy Carter, who appointed him to be the first African American US ambassador to the United Nations. Carter and Andrew are looking in the opposite direction as Dr. King, at a perpendicular wall lined with black-and-white photos of family and friends. These are hung above an overwhelmed bookcase, with volumes stacked both horizontally and vertically. Resting on the bookcase is Jonathan Alter's Carter biography *His Very Best: Jimmy Carter, a Life*, as well as a mounted medal, although I can't make out through the hazy interface whether it's Andrew's Presidential Medal of Freedom or his Legion of Honour.

It was an intimidating setup, never mind the fact that he was reluctant to speak with me at all.

"I mean, I really tried my best to get out of this," he admitted.

Despite all the awards and recognitions, all the larger-than-life figures he's worked alongside and befriended, Andrew is incredibly humble. He said he's "not blessed with organizational skills," even though his strategic maneuvering before the Birmingham campaign was essential to its impact on the civil rights movement. He also told me he didn't want to talk about Greenwood because he doesn't know much about it. Of course, I didn't want to talk about the bank with him. I wanted to talk about the context surrounding the bank: the nature of economic revolution and the decision to fight capitalism by engaging it, rather than eradicating it as most other revolutionary ideas had proposed.

"Capitalism has worked for us," he said. "Any system is capable of being creative and visionary."

In 1981, at the urging of Dr. King's widow, Coretta Scott King, Andrew ran for mayor of Atlanta with a "public purpose capitalism" platform. He vowed to develop the city and increase jobs without using taxpayer funds. He proposed new highways and an airport, developments that brought in 1,100 new businesses, $70 billion in private investments, and more than 1 million new jobs by the end of his two terms as mayor.

"We went straight to Wall Street," he said. "We probably haven't used a penny of taxpayer money since 1974."

Andrew also saw the benefits of private funding when he helped bring the 1996 Olympic Games to Atlanta. Toward the end of his tenure as mayor, he was approached by Billy Payne, a young real estate attorney, about the idea.

"Billy Payne had a dream," Andrew told me, rather cheekily.

Payne, who has said he was driven by a fear of dying young after suffering a heart attack at twenty-six and needing a triple bypass at thirty-four, had started going to church—enter the Spirit of Atlanta—and watched 16 Days of Glory, a documentary about the 1984 Games in Los Angeles. He wanted the Games in Atlanta. Most of Andrew's staffers were adamantly against the idea, because recent host cities like Montreal were buried in hundreds of millions of dollars in debt from the event. But Andrew had a sweet spot for the Olympics, recalling memories of his father taking him to see a replay of Jesse Owens's gold-medal run at the 1936 Games when Andrew was just a boy.

Out of office and free of municipal naysayers, Andrew took on the Olympic campaign alongside Payne. Again he went to the private sector, raising $1.7 billion to fund the games. What money the commission did raise from federal, state, and local contributions (about $500 million) went directly into the community, paying for road improvements, streetscaping, an expansion of the airport, residential rehabilitation and development, and commercial revitalization.

The Atlanta Games prep did have its shortcomings. Months ahead of the Olympics, the city erected a 1,100-bed detention center while simultaneously adopting new policies that criminalized the homeless population. When $5 million of the "revitalization" funds was allotted to Woodruff Park, a longtime safe haven for people experiencing homelessness, the vast majority of the people there were swept into the new city jail, hidden away before the world's eye focused on Atlanta for the Games. The Atlanta City Detention Center continues to function as a jail, despite ongoing efforts by community organizers to close it.

Andrew still sees securing and producing the Atlanta Games as a glowing example of capitalism gone right. To refute the notion that it was maybe not so good for poor Atlantans, he points to the $19 million profit the Games brought to downtown. This financial boost has allowed organizations like the Atlanta Neighborhood Development Partnership, he said, to build or rehabilitate 1,300 affordable housing units in neighborhoods near the newly constructed venues.[17]

"What we had left over at the end of the Olympics, we saw to it that minorities and family-owned businesses got 41 percent of everything that we built," he said.

Andrew brings an echo into the boardroom at Greenwood: an echo from lessons learned during the 1960s campaigns for equality; an echo of Dr. King's call for nonviolent rebellions; even his mayoral motto "public purpose capitalism" influenced the fifteen-year-old activist who walked into his office all those years ago.

"I practice what I would consider to be 'compassionate capitalism,'" Killer Mike told me, putting an alliterative spin on Andrew's mayoral platform. "I don't want corporations to own all the apartments and multi-units that my wife and I own, because they're not sensitive to people who are looking for affordable housing. I rent to people who look like me and my sisters when we grew up and were working in the city."

"I am a capitalist because I don't want to simply be a victim of capitalism," he said.

Greenwood's desire to both embrace capitalism and betray its current application and form is driven by its founders' visions of "purpose" and "compassion." These are important caveats, they say, because in a society that's interpreted capitalism to mean "every person for themselves," the idea of adding purpose and compassion to the mix does, indeed, seem radical.

Into the Unknown

Atlanta is a city with numerous forms of protests: It was where Dr. King's vehicle for coordinating nonviolent demonstrations across the nation, the Southern Christian Leadership Conference, was born. Its educational protest takes the form of four higher education institutions reserved for Black students, one of the least represented groups in American colleges and universities.[18] An economic protest like Greenwood's fits into the rebellious fabric of the city like a single stitch in a vast tapestry.

Since the launch of its site in 2022, the bank has made two key acquisitions that have expanded its reach. In May 2022 Greenwood announced the acquisition of the Gathering Spot, a membership-based community of Black and Latino professionals, creatives, and entrepreneurs with brick-and-mortar locations in Atlanta, Washington, DC, and Los Angeles, as well as offshoots in New York City, Chicago, Detroit, Charlotte, and Houston. The Gathering Spot cofounder and CEO Ryan Wilson was named chief community officer at Greenwood, and the team estimates the combined community of

Greenwood account holders and the Gathering Spot members is over 1 million people.

A month after the Gathering Spot announcement, Greenwood acquired Valence, a development platform for Black professionals that has tens of thousands of job listings and career opportunities. The three deals, according to the bank's press office, have created "a trifecta of fintech product, million member community, and career development platform."[19]

In addition to strategic acquisitions, Greenwood penned a name, image, and likeness deal with Travis Hunter, the number one overall college football recruit in the 2021–2022 season. Hunter became the highest-ranked prospect to ever commit to an HBCU when he chose to enroll at Jackson State University; now he is the face of Greenwood's "Choose Black" campaign, which encourages people to support Black businesses, schools, and causes.

"By choosing to join forces with Greenwood, I am again highlighting the strength of the Black community in collaborating and partnering," Hunter said in a release announcing his role as a Greenwood brand ambassador. "I want the next generation to feel empowered to make the right choices and support Black businesses and Black excellence. I'm inspired by what Greenwood is doing to support financial freedom for minorities."[20]

As for its founders, Ryan Glover is still steering the everyday operations of the company and serves as its primary PR machine, explaining the ins and outs of the venture to the press and curious parties like myself. Killer Mike continues to promote Greenwood on social media and in public appearances, but he has spent much of his time since the bank's launch in the studio, and released his sixth studio album, *MICHAEL*, in 2023. His first solo record in over a decade, the album is an homage to "the civil rights movement, the abolitionist movement, which gave us some of the most beautiful music ever," he told Hypebeast.[21]

Andrew Young, at ninety-one years of age, has seen a lot of ups and downs when it comes to progress. After winning reelection for mayor in 1985, he announced to supporters, "I am glad to be mayor of this city, where once the mayor had me thrown in jail."[22] He's lived through the assassination of one of his closest friends and long enough to see Dr. King's vision reverberate decades beyond his death. He's seen Atlanta go from a city whose 1917 city planner Robert Whitten wrote, "A reasonable segregation is normal, inevitable and desirable,"[23] to an international city, with eighteen Fortune 100 companies—including Coca-Cola, Home Depot, UPS, Delta Air Lines, AT&T Mobility, and Newell Rubbermaid—headquartered there.[24]

Greenwood bank hopes to be this kind of equal but opposite reaction to what was eventually the downfall of its namesake. The Greenwood district thrived for over two decades until, in 1921, a Black shoe shiner in Tulsa was accused of raping a white elevator operator. A feverish white mob descended on Greenwood, killing 300 residents and detaining 6,000 more in internment camps. The Tulsa Race Massacre lasted for two days, left 35 blocks of grocery stores, restaurants, and drug stores in ashes, and rendered nearly 10,000 residents homeless. Although there was some rebuilding in subsequent years, insurance companies refused to pay damage claims, and a new fire ordinance was enacted to prevent Black owners from independent building. Due to the sheer magnitude of the devastation and the barriers to rebuilding that followed, the town never fully recovered.[25]

I asked Andrew about Greenwood not just as an inspiration but as a cautionary tale. Was the idea of a Black Wall Street too good to be true? If not, what made this moment different?

"Just 100 years of effort," he retorted.

Through various diversification efforts—like the one Maynard Jackson forced in Atlanta banks—and cultural advancements, such as the rise of rap and hip-hop, there have been many successful economic campaigns in the Black community. Mike points to the rise of Cadillac cars to exemplify the kind of power Black Americans can exert with buying power.

"Had it not been for Black people's want to buy Cadillac cars, we would not have Cadillac cars today," he asserts. "At one point Cadillac would not sell to Black people. Once Cadillac lifted that shadow ban of sorts, Cadillac sales flourished, Cadillac became one of the more popular brands, and I would even argue in matters of SUVs and trucks now, had it not been for hip-hop and their making an icon of the Cadillac Escalades, I doubt you would have Cadillac so prominent in the truck market today. Well, that happens more if you take care of your individual and community finances and when your community participates in the bigger world economy."

Although their mission and messaging around Black empowerment through capital are aligned, the three cofounders are very different. Shoulder-to-shoulder they look like Goldilocks's three bears, with Mike a head taller than the rest, the crown of Andrew's head just reaching Mike's bicep, and Ryan bridging the vertical gap between them. They're also inspired by different movements from the past, Andrew taking cues from his friend Dr. King, while Mike tends to exude a more Malcolm X vibe, even sampling Malcolm's "Who Are You?" speech in his track "Pressure." But like the variety of artistic techniques that line the Beltline underpass, the men's theories of change blend seamlessly to move a new generation of activists who are beginning to see the merits of both missions. Their politics are not in conflict. Rather, they harmonize like the rhythmic beats of a single track.

These seeming contradictions are not unfamiliar to Andrew, who's seen his fair share of life's tendency to present us with both all that is good and all that is evil. His life has been filled with bright stars and dark days, liberation and death, prosperity and famine. None of it makes much sense, he conceded. Why would the Olympics come to Atlanta? Why would a rapper and an activist go in on a bank? Why would a city in the Deep South be the hub for HBCUs? Why would millions of Africans be made cargo, then trade, then slaves?

The answers fall into Andrew's long list of "unknowns." But in a sitdown with Mike on his WABE Atlanta show "Love & Respect with

Killer Mike," Andrew offered an interesting hypothesis for that last question.

"We may have been sent here by God to make this nation be what it ought to be."

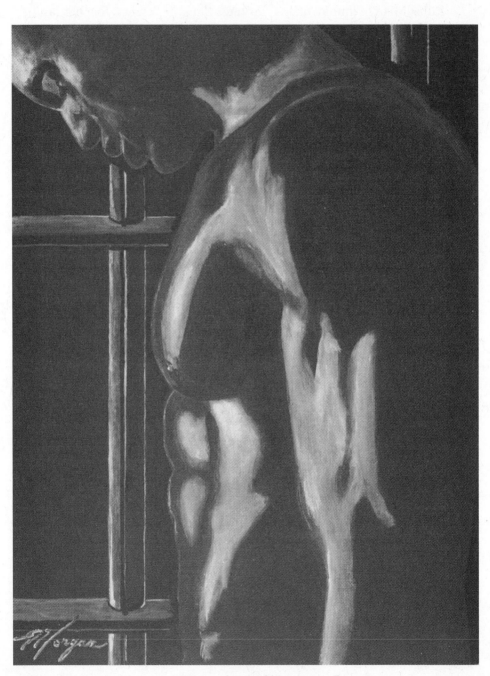

Doing Time by Gerald Morgan

6

Reimagining Infrastructure:

The Autonomous Infrastructure Mission (AIM)

« S ista Paula."

His voice was deep and mellow. It reminded me of Frantz Fanon's introduction to *Black Skin, White Masks* where he wrote, "Things I'm going to say, not shout. I've long given up on shouting."[1] The voice on the other end of the call echoed through a long hallway he just finished mopping. It came through scratchy, a common side effect of old-school pay phones still mounted to the walls of Kern Valley State Prison.

I was getting quite fond of Heshima Denham calling me "sista." His expression of intimacy reminded me that we are bonded by a connective tissue deeper than race.

"'Shima, how you holding up?" I replied.

A correctional officer positioned some distance from the pay-phone barked an order. It bounced off the walls and reverberated through the phone. Prison is intentionally disorientating, as I am constantly aware, whether it be the prerecorded messages that interrupt my conversations with Heshima and Ivan every few minutes or the irregular schedules we work around to communicate. No matter how many years you've been inside—Heshima has been incarcerated since 1994—you never get used to it.

"Disorienting tactics allow prison officials to alter inmates' views, beliefs, and realities," writes political scientist Patrick Doolittle in his senior thesis for Yale University, the basis for the Marshall Project's Emmy-nominated series *The Zo*.[2] "They do away with structures, traditions, worldviews, and logic that may empower them, or keep them tethered to reality itself."

I first reached out to Heshima after learning about Amend the 13th, an organization he developed in prison to oppose the slavery exception in the US Constitution. In researching an article, I discovered a recording of a speech Heshima had made for the August 2017 Millions for Prisoners March, where activists from around the country descended on Washington DC to protest inhumane prison conditions and the 13th Amendment's slavery provision. One of the country's last remaining Black-owned radical periodicals, the *San Francisco Bay View*, helped galvanize support for the demonstration in the Bay Area and posted Heshima's speech on its website.

"From the slave codes to the Black codes, to the legal slavery provision of the 13th Amendment and the thousands of civil death statutes that derive their legal authority therefrom, America has made a mockery of the concept of 'freedom and justice for all' by ensuring it is always denied to some," his speech went.[3]

I wrote to him at Kern Valley State Prison to ask if he'd be interested in contributing an article about the 13th Amendment for an upcoming issue of the All of Us or None newspaper. After several replies were confiscated by guards, he called me.

"I'm doing OK, you know? Can't complain," he said.

He most certainly could complain, but that's not really his style. With each new evolution of punishment and deprivation he's endured, Heshima has held firm to his humanity and identity. He does this by using his New Afrikan name, Joka Heshima Denham—rather than his government name, Shannon Denham—*Heshima* stemming from the Swahili word *sima*, meaning respect and honor, and *Joka* referring to Hô Chí Minh's "dragon," a being that would fly out of the prison gates upon the dismantlement of imperialism.[4]

He also makes stylistic choices in his writing to maintain a sense of autonomy. In his articles for publications from the *Bay View* to *Mother Jones*, he critiques "Amerika" or "Amerikkka"—the single *K* standing for "killer," he says, and the KKK being fairly obvious—calling attention to the 50 million Indigenous people killed during western expansion and the 250 million Africans who died en route to the New World.

"It's a way for my reader to see a term and not associate it with what the current zeitgeist associates the term with, but instead its function and purpose," Heshima told me. "The underlying basis of law in this nation is violence and death.

"There's also a more rebellious motive associated with how men like me express ourselves. Words are instruments of power."

To exert that power, Heshima writes prolifically and provocatively. He's written about America's devolution into "the most advanced fascist state in human history," rising above Mussolini's Italy and Hitler's Germany, made possible through both advanced technology and a more cunning ability to disguise itself as noble in its actions.[5] This can be seen in the many Big Brother spy tactics it deploys in the name of national security. Cloaked in this camouflaged persona as a gatekeeper of peace and security, the United States can claim to be the world's safeguard of liberty while having its population heavily surveilled and more prisoners per capita than any other nation. Domestically, its deception is even more profound, evolving and advancing oppressive systems that impact a compliant population that yearns for the status quo and is conditioned against revolution.

"When I speak of fascism, I'm talking about the assimilation of billions of people to a particular psychology," Heshima once told me. "It's a psychology that rationalizes stuff like having more than enough housing to house every single person inside this country, yet callously allowing millions of people to sleep on the street; that claims to be the beacon of freedom and justice yet has the largest prison population on the planet."

Perhaps the greatest validation of the power of Heshima's words comes in the form of the consequences they've earned him in prison. The most severe of these consequences were inflicted during his time at Pelican Bay State Prison in Crescent City, California, in the early 2000s. Heshima began receiving 1819 forms, the corrections department's "Notification of Disapproval," and his mail would go missing. Next came a slew of Form 115s, the department's disciplinary report. These seemed to correlate less with actual violations and more with how outspoken he was becoming about his New Afrikan Revolutionary Nationalists beliefs, an ideology stemming from Marxism, Leninism, Maoism, and Black revolutionary tradition. Eventually, the department used a tattoo he had, his possession of *Blood in My Eye*, and a drawing he had made as "evidence" of an affiliation with a prison gang and sent him to what was termed a "validated security housing unit (SHU)," an area where prisoners who were accused of being gang members were held in solitary confinement indefinitely unless they were paroled or "debriefed" by defecting from the gang and providing incriminating information about its members. As prisoners in Pelican Bay put it: "Parole, snitch, or die."[6]

The prison department justified its use of indeterminate solitary by claiming prison gangs were responsible for rampant violence and drug sales within the system. In response to criticism, the prison warden at the time, Clark Ducart, was quoted as saying, "You gotta keep the predators away from the prey."[7]

The "predator" reference, an age-old racist trope, lends itself to the argument that prisoners are not seen as people. But more significantly, this wide-cast dragnet of gang suspicion allowed correctional officers and prison administrators to control the proliferation of *ideas* under the pretense of controlling contraband. To the prison department, ideas carry just as much danger, if not more, than alleged gang beefs or drug use. This position was no more apparent than an instance in 2012 when four men, allegedly from the four biggest rival gangs inside California's prison system, penned a joint letter calling for a ceasefire in the name of cooperation. They gave it to administrators and asked them to proliferate it. After all, they were being kept in the SHU for instigating violence, and this was a call to end it. Prison officials confiscated the statement and destroyed it: Apparently, the idea of prisoners working together was far more foreboding than the population killing itself off.[8]

On Our Own

At the time of the joint letter, Heshima was already deep in the underbelly of Pelican Bay. He had been "validated" as a member of the Black Guerrilla Family, a Black collective that Heshima says has been strategically misconstrued as a gang to prevent its true values from being legitimized.

"I was back there in the SHU with them for twenty years and they wasn't stabbing nobody, or selling drugs, or any of that crap they tried to put out into the public," Heshima said, his voice still calm and measured. "They were there reading books and articles and teaching the younger brothers."

Affiliations aside, *no one*, gang member or otherwise, deserves what the United Nations' Special Rapporteur on Torture called "the severe and often irreparable psychological and physical consequences of solitary confinement."[9] Prisoners in these units were kept in their cells for twenty-three hours a day, only leaving to exercise in isolation in small rooms, divided by concrete walls.

"In the most inhumane conditions that can be produced in an industrialized nation, an indeterminate SHU, a torture unit, these men who had no hope of ever getting out understood something," Heshima told me. "If we are going to end legal slavery in America, we'd have to liberate ourselves."

This idea of self-liberation would ultimately lead to Heshima's blueprint for the Autonomous Infrastructure Mission (AIM), a design for self-supported communities independent of the state. According to its mission statement: "If the institutions which have preserved legal slavery in Amerika continue to be the primary basis of the infrastructure in our communities, the social ills they inevitably produce will continue to perpetuate de facto 'legal' dehumanization and exploitation."

Heshima needed empirical evidence that self-liberation was possible, and he wouldn't have to wait long, as the same men who had penned the ceasefire letter had already begun developing a plan for freedom.

The four men at the far end, also called the Short Corridor due to its remoteness, were Todd Ashker, Sitawa Jamaa, Arturo Castellanos, and Antonio Guillen. They had been isolated together because the department believed they were high-ranking gang members, with sway over the Aryan Brotherhood, the Black Guerrilla Family, the Mexican Mafia, and Nuestra Familia, respectively. With little more than a food slot to shout through and cracks in the concrete wall between exercise spaces to relay messages, an unlikely collaboration between the men from rival groups began to form. They redefined their caste, putting themselves in a prisoner "class" rather than in racial enclaves. In 2011 they staged two modest hunger strikes, mostly to test their grit, calculating how much water they needed to keep their hearts working and how much weight they would lose. They spent the next year putting on weight and coordinating with advocacy groups, friends, and family through coded letters and notations in law books to spread the word about the strike. On July 8, 2013, the first day of the strike, 30,000 California prisoners stopped eating.[10] The fast lasted fifty-nine days and eventually led to a federal class-action suit that ended indeterminate sentencing in California.[11]

Back on the phone, a loud noise interrupted the conversation. The guard's voice, closer this time, muttered something to Heshima, who seemed to be covering the bottom of the handset.

"Hey, I gotta wheel a guy to medical," he said when he finished with the guard. "Lemme call you right back."

I was reminded that the liberation Heshima and his fellow hunger strikers earned is limited. When Heshima was released from the SHU back into the general population, he found himself at Kern Valley State Prison, an eleven-hour drive from where he started at Pelican Bay. There he works as a porter, mopping hallways, transporting men to the infirmary, and doing routine maintenance. While it may seem counterintuitive to engage in the system of prison labor rather than resist it, Heshima has been told that refusal to work would land him back in the SHU. Although he acknowledges that the plan he developed in solitary for AIM may not be contingent on his freedom, it is contingent on his ability to communicate with those he's entrusted with carrying out his mission.

A Labor of Love

Bri Hawkins grew up bouncing around youth homes in the Midwest. Amid a chaotic upbringing, the children who were raised together came to depend primarily on each other. Bri often speaks of those she lived with as her brothers and sisters.

As is common with those placed in group homes—youth in this environment are two and a half times more likely to become involved in the justice system[12]—Bri and her contemporaries began engaging with what Heshima calls the "underground economy," a criminalized series of ventures that the unemployed, the uneducated, and the consistently denied participate in for survival.

"If you don't have a job, or there's no capital to fund an entrepreneurial enterprise, there's only one place you can actually make money, and that's the underground economy," Heshima explained. "It's the doorway to a very unique aspect of American culture where the system denies access, pushes people into the underground, then criminalizes that means of survival."

It was here in the underground that Bri's radicalization formed. When she was thirteen, she was living in another group home, this one in Chicago. One afternoon a group of kids from the home engaged in a robbery. They dispersed as the police arrived, Bri and her assumed brother Dante dodging into an alley. Dante, a young Black teen who was unarmed, was attempting to scale a fence when a police officer shot him in the back. Bri watched as his lifeless body fell to the ground.

"That's kind of what sparked my radicalization," Bri said. "It was definitely a transformative incident in my life."

After Dante's death, Bri started engaging in community protests surrounding police homicide and police brutality. She stood with the families of Mike Brown and George Floyd and connected with groups like Families United, a nonprofit that travels the country providing support to families and survivors of police violence. She also connected with various prison abolition groups. (The parallels between police brutality and the dehumanization of Black Americans via incarceration provide much crossover for orgs in this space.) Bri began following social media accounts such as the one operated by Jailhouse Lawyers Speak, a prisoner-led organization that fights for humane conditions and the preservation of human rights in carceral settings. In addition to organizing inside—providing law books and courses to prisoners across the US— Jailhouse Lawyers Speak has a prolific outreach program, and back in 2019, its Facebook page featured information about Heshima's blueprint for self-liberation that linked out to a website. As she read the details of Amend the 13th and the Autonomous Infrastructure Mission, Bri's eyes began to widen.

"I was sitting at these protests watching the same attempts of things trying to be done in the community to effect change and knowing that a piece was missing," Bri said. "This was the missing piece."

Bri used the website's contact form to request more information and connected with Adam Brashere, the national coordinator for AIM.

"Some activists are lip service: they print flyers, but they do little work," Adam said. "The more time I spent with Bri, I saw she was sincere and that she had a way of sharing our mission with the people in a way they could understand."

For Bri to start an AIM chapter in Grand Rapids, Michigan, where she had established residency, she needed to be walked through the platform: an aggregation of eight distinct community programs designed to eliminate dependency on mainstream power structures.

The Sustainable Agricultural Commune provides access to healthy foods and restores urban ecologies.

The Closed-Circuit Economic Initiative creates collective ownership of businesses and promotes economic circulation within the bounds of the autonomous community.

The Youth Community Action Program and the New Afrikan Math and Science Centers Initiative focus on developing the next generation, educating them on their cultural history and how to further the AIM when their time comes to lead.

The Emergency Response Network provides training and guidelines for responding to community crises, whether a natural disaster or a domestic disturbance.

The Community Safe-Zones Initiative preserves a sense of security for youth, women, and elders, providing shelter and necessities.

The integrity of these zones is protected by the Secure Communities Mandate, which trains community members to serve as a defense force.

The Strategic Release Initiative calls for decarceration, specifically the release of influential elders within the Black liberation ecosystem.

All of these work in conjunction with the Amend the 13th: Abolish "Legal" Slavery in Amerika Movement, a coalition-based national campaign to remove the slavery provision from the 13th Amendment and repeal all civil death laws. The AIM is where oppressed people, enslaved under the 13th Amendment, would find refuge upon release from bondage.

"Amend the 13th is saying you cannot begin to end the institutions upon which legal slavery rests in this country without first abolishing its existence in law," Adam explained to me. "AIM is saying there is another way of life—that we can police and defend ourselves, that we can educate and feed ourselves—and in so that new way of life you no longer risk falling prey to the trap of the underground."

While Adam trained Bri on the elements of AIM, she began a dialogue with Heshima directly about history, context, and a deep love of "the people," those suffering under, and sometimes participating in, oppressive power structures. They spoke every day, and from their collective love blossomed a deep love for each other. They became engaged in March 2023.

"Our bond is something like no other," Bri said. "We bonded through our love for the people and the struggle that we both willingly fight in every day."

What was it exactly, I wanted to know, that Bri fell in love with? Was it Heshima's tall and toned body? His subtle smile—the kind where only one side rises—of a clever man who's found self-liberation in an environment of deprivation? Was it the brain she picked for inspiration and a deeper understanding of the intricate plan for communal liberation?

"It's his heart," Bri said. "With all the sacrifices he's made and everything he's done for the people . . . he's just a remarkable man."

Like Father, Like Son

Heshima, as previously indicated, is well-read and has developed many aspects of the AIM based on critical analyses of writers like Frantz Fanon, the Black Panther Party's Fred Hampton, and George Jackson.

"If I picked up George's torch from where it was laying in his blood and I carried it to 2023—with all the technological advances we've had since then—it would look like AIM," he once told me.

But perhaps his greatest inspiration came from someone closer to home: his father.

In fact, Dudley Denham could have been synonymous with "home" for Heshima. The family moved around a lot when Dudley served in the air force, and Heshima's mother died by suicide when he was still a baby, likely suffering from postpartum depression at a time when such a thing was misunderstood. Although Dudley remarried eventually, he was the only constant parental figure and role model in Heshima's life.

After Dudley's military service concluded, he found work at a Ford plant near Lake Michigan and began engaging in Black liberation movements. He joined Jesse Jackson's Operation PUSH (People United to Serve Humanity) and the Black Panther Party, offering his home as a meeting space. In the basement, Heshima sat beside his father as elders, donning black leather jackets, berets, and gloves, outlined the Panthers' ten-point program and told stories about a time when Blacks were kings and queens.

"It made an indelible mark on my mind," Heshima said. "I learned at a very young age—and I'm talking like six or seven years old—that self-determination and self-sufficiency had to be the primary objectives of any people seeking to be truly free."

Heshima saw his father emerge from these meetings with concrete plans on how to implement community uplift from within. His daughter Duvon, Heshima's older sister, remembers her father rallying workers at the Ford factory to ensure every family in the community had a feast on Thanksgiving and presents for the children on Christmas. It's a fond memory of Dudley, who died in 2012, kept sacred by his daughter.

"Back in the sixties and seventies, people didn't have a lot, so our communities worked together," Duvon recalled. "Now, people try to 'elevate' to new communities and leave the old neighborhood to just deteriorate."

The deterioration among neighborhoods that had been previously segregated and neglected during Jim Crow was a constant everywhere the family moved, whether it be Gary, Indiana, where Duvon spent most of her childhood, or Jackson, Mississippi, where Heshima spent his. From a historical perspective, this is likely an effect of blockbusting, a practice that profited real estate agents in a post–World War II segregationist society. Using psychologically manipulative tactics, like hiring Black women to walk neighborhoods with a baby carriage or buying entire developments only to leave them empty and give the appearance of a slum, agents and developers convinced white residents to sell their homes at below-market prices, then sold those homes at inflated prices to Black families.[13] This strategy preyed on preexisting biases around desegregated neighborhoods, provoked so-called white flight, and reinforced the myth that housing prices fall when Black people move into a neighborhood—it created a situation that would ensure that outcome. In these neighborhoods, all the money that could have been spent on community development or advancement was frontloaded to the purchase of a home.

"Falling sale prices in neighborhoods where blockbusters created white panic was deemed as proof by the [Federal Housing Authority] that property values would decline if African Americans moved in," Richard Rothstein points out. "But if the agency had not adopted a discriminatory and unconstitutional racial policy, African Americans would have been able, like whites, to locate throughout metropolitan areas rather than attempting to establish presence in only a few blockbuster communities, and speculators would not have been able to prey on white fears that their neighborhoods would soon turn from all white to all black."[14]

The decline of subdivisions within the bounds of metropolitan areas was acutely felt by Heshima in Jackson, Mississippi, a place he somewhat affectionately calls "a ghetto's ghetto." The majority of his childhood was spent in a family home across the street from former slave quarters that had been converted into shotgun houses for people one economical step ahead of the unhoused. Jackson is where Heshima learned about the underground economy and about the world he was born into.

"I grew up with the understanding that, from a historical standpoint, I live in a society that has built institutions and structures which were not meant for me," Heshima said. "That unbroken lineage of oppression, it really screams out at you in a place like Jackson."

Heshima ultimately followed his father's example and joined the military, undergoing intensive training to become a member of Seal Team Four in San Diego, California. He was discharged after a bar fight that started when a Marine called him a racial slur and took a swing at him. Heshima won the fight but lost the privilege of remaining in the military. Once he was booted from the Navy, he was alone in California with a skill set that didn't translate well to the civilian sector.

"There was nowhere to be a military equipment operator outside the military," Heshima said. "There was nothing for me in the mainstream US economy, but the underground economy provided a veritable cornucopia of opportunities."

By design, Heshima's new mode of survival—participation in the underground economy—landed him in front of a judge. Though he'd never been convicted of a crime previously, the state made up for lost time by piling on a laundry list of charges. Duvon and Dudley sat in the courtroom as the sentence was read: an indeterminate sentence of twenty-five years to life.

"The last thing my dad said to his son was, 'I'll see you later, son,'" Duvon said as the painful memory choked her speech. "He was in shackles, and that's the last thing my father said to my brother."

After a brief moment of tear-shedding, she continued steadfastly.

"My brother shouldn't be in there, and anyone who knows him knows he shouldn't," she said. "You can't really have feelings in there, but I know it hurts Shannon because it hurts me every day, that memory of their last interaction."

Trial and Tribulation

After he entered the prison system in 1994, Heshima became a prolif-
erator of Black liberation politics. He also continued to learn, associ-
ating with the New Afrikan revolutionaries who complemented his
knowledge of Jackson and Fanon with Mao and Dr. Frances Cress
Welsing.

"With each book, with each text, each talk, I began to get a clear
perception of both the system I lived in and my relationship to it, and I
got a greater understanding of the historical ideology and the oppression that we suffer every day," Heshima said. "In fact, it got worse . . .
the desire to know. I had to know so I could change the social reality of
myself, my people, and all of humanity."

The philosophy contained in these texts, combined with the values
he learned from his father and lessons from the Pelican Bay hunger
strike, helped Heshima create the Autonomous Infrastructure Mission. Working with Adam, his connection to the world outside prison,
he began looking for leaders and regions where the elements of AIM
could be implemented.

There were fits and starts in various locations around the country;
Duvon, who lives near Dallas, struggled to find a community partner.
("As far as donations of time and resources . . . they don't like that very
much here," she told me). Other individuals pegged as "coordinators"
turned out to be more of the "lip service" types Adam bemoaned. But
in Grand Rapids, AIM took root—quite literally.

It began with community surveys, which Bri and some local volunteers distributed to residents in Heartside and Baxter in 2019. The
neighborhoods are unique, both in relation to Grand Rapids itself and
to each other. Heartside, a neighborhood in downtown, once had a
large African American community but now consists only of 11 percent Black homeowners or renters. It also counts five city missions
within its borders, which provide temporary shelter to the numerous
residents who were displaced after the neighborhood underwent gentrification.[15] Baxter, located in the southeast region of the city, is still

a near-majority African American (41 percent) neighborhood with middle- and low-income families.[16]

When the surveys came back, Bri discovered a dominant interest in the Sustainable Agriculture Commune among residents from both communities.

"One of the biggest concerns was food stability," Bri said. "For many residents in these neighborhoods, the closest store is the minute mart down the street, where there aren't a lot of options for fresh produce and healthy food."

She began connecting with local nonprofits and sought material donations from places like Ace Hardware. Bri and several volunteers familiar with AIM—a collective of roughly fifty individuals—used the donations to create "grow boxes," planters contained within wood planks. Twenty-three families have signed on to "host" these grow boxes, tending to the garden, distributing the food to the most needy members of the community, and rotating with volunteers to cook meals made of surplus food for upward of 100 families who congregate every Monday for the AIM soup kitchen.

According to the AIM charter, each contributor to the agricultural commune—whether contributing financially or in the form of labor—is part of its collective ownership, entitling them to 50 percent of the produce and 50 percent of dividends. While the preliminary focus of the agriculture commune in Grand Rapids has been to feed the community, Heshima's outline envisions the commune selling 50 percent of its produce at farmers' markets once the program has scaled up.

"The ultimate goal is closed economics," Bri explained. "Once the SAC gets off the ground, we'll be able to buy our own land and build our own businesses."

Other elements of AIM have also been enacted in Grand Rapids including the Community Safe-Zone, a site, according to Heshima's plan, "where Our Youth, Women and Elders can go about the daily activities of social life without the fear of violent death, assault or abduction." The CSZ embodies several programs within the AIM ecosystem, and the Grand Rapids zone was a kind of pilot program for what AIM on a larger scale might look like. Like the preliminary hunger strikes in Pelican Bay, the Grand Rapids CSZ became a test of grit, and a teacher of hard-earned lessons.

Bri and other AIM members established an autonomous zone in a section of Heartside Park in 2020 by setting up tents to serve as a food pantry, sleeping quarters, showers, and social service areas. The Heartside residents who had been pushed into tent cities, shelters, or dilapidated homes were invited to seek refuge within the zone, the only rule being no hard drugs allowed within its boundaries. The CSZ operated similarly to Occupy movement spaces, particularly the George Floyd Square occupation in Minneapolis, where concrete barriers were erected to protect protestors.[17] Rather than walls, the Grand Rapids community implemented another component of AIM: the Secure Communities Mandate, a trained security force charged with protecting the integrity and safety of people within the autonomous zone.

Volunteers who had been vetted and who had attended an eight-month de-escalation course, settled disagreements within the boundaries of the CSZ, but the outer perimeter was guarded by the Secure Communities Mandate. For two months, the Mandate held the space designated as the Safe-Zone, pacing the boundary in black, bulletproof vests with walkie-talkies clipped to the shoulder straps. Some wore black berets, an homage to the Panthers. Some were armed, while others had trained in martial arts and did not carry a weapon.

The defense force's mettle was put to the test as soon as the autonomous zone was established at Heartside Park. Almost daily, they stood face-to-face with police in military-grade riot gear, but they outnumbered the cops by a large enough margin to stave off any confrontation. Instead, the police department tracked their schedules, watching them from nearby rooftops, and waited to infiltrate until the defensive line had thinned. When that moment came, almost sixty days after the zone had been established, fifty militarized officers tore down tents, destroyed or confiscated supplies, and threw people in jail for charges ranging from obstruction to trespassing. Bri was not on-site that day, so she, as she puts it, "unfortunately" did not get arrested. Instead, she received sixteen tickets for minor infractions, such as refusal to leave and feeding the unhoused.

In the wake of the destruction, the city's first order of business was to charge as many people as it could with criminal actions. For Bri and the Mandate, safely relocating the 100 or so individuals who needed safe housing was top of mind. They rented U-Hauls to transport both people and belongings for those who had either come off the streets or left an unsafe living environment, but the police tailed the vehicles and blocked public access roads.

"We had to rent those U-Hauls for three days because we couldn't get through," Bri said.

I asked Bri what kind of lessons she learned from the Safe-Zone and its ultimate demise. Was there something the community could have done differently, or was it just bad timing?

"It's always the right time for the Community Safe-Zone," she replied. "Unity is our path to power, but it only works with all hands on deck."

"When we restructure, it will need to be an impenetrable space," she continued. "We need to make it impenetrable with community participation, safety patrol, and controlling the resources and people moving in and out."

Infiltration is something Heshima and most activists in this space are keenly aware of, though not many organizations have learned the lesson to the point of implementing a counteroffensive. All local AIM coordinators receive a detailed analysis of COINTELPRO tactics, including a note to *expect* infiltration and potential criminalization of AIM initiatives. This explicit effort to curb intrusions is complemented by a covert vetting process in which potential members or coordinators are sent a questionnaire and current members fact-check their answers.

"Anyone who has done a cursory examination of history under-stands the depths and the lengths the ruling class will go to destroy movements that have the potential to create fundamental change," Heshima said. "You won't get far in transforming the nature of a soci-ety if you don't think in terms of protecting the structures you build."

As of this writing, Bri is still looking for a location to rebuild the Community Safe-Zone. In the meantime, she's begun implementing some of AIM's youth initiatives. The Grand Rapids Youth Community Action Program has been offering school-age children free after-school political education classes and unity-building workshops. One project that was particularly successful asked youth participants to come up with their own community surveys, distribute them to their local peers, and come up with action plans based on the responses.

"Their eyes lit up because they were understanding how they could connect to the community," Bri said.

While Bri seems to be constantly engaged in AIM—responding to community crises like the loss of the Safe-Zone, harvesting produce from the grow boxes, or empowering the next generation—she does have a day job. She bartends at a local pub, picking up extra shifts if needed to make ends meet.

"We're forced to participate in this fascist system for survival until everything in AIM comes together," Bri said. "Revolution is grasping problems at the root, taking everything you see and the social effects and analyzing it to prevent it from happening again. A full disconnect from the system might be years down the road, but the importance of planting the seed and educating the youth on developing these elements of a new system are essential to our liberation as people."

Concrete Conditions

Although a prolific writer, Shima has a way of saying a lot with a little. For example, we got into a conversation about critical race theory once, and before I could finish my question, he inadvertently chuckled.

"Yeah, critical race *theory*," he said. "How come when they talk about anyone else's past it's 'history,' but my past is theoretical?"

Pretty much sums it up, doesn't it?

To move beyond the realm of the theoretical, I asked Heshima about crime and punishment in the context of a fully enacted AIM. I knew he was too intelligent and realistic to envision a utopia, but

I asked him anyway. Was there no punishment in AIM because the structures had extinguished the fires that fuel criminalization?

Heshima, expectedly, rejected the idea of a utopian society and laid out two groups of offenders based on the level of harm their crime may inflict: reparable and irreparable.

"There are a number of restorative justice methods that can be used to correct behavior contrary to the values of the community without the person needing to be purged from society itself," Heshima explained. "But if someone goes so far as to rape a sister or murder someone, they might need to be exiled."

I pounced.

"That sounds like a fine line to walk," I said. "I mean, in my mind, *you're* in exile, so any system that includes exile would simply be a regurgitation of the oppressive system you worked to free yourself from. How do you reconcile that?"

Oh man, I was so proud of myself. I thought I'd out-abolitioned a true abolitionist. It was short-lived.

"Prison is an irrational punishment because incapacitation makes redemption and reparations impossible," Heshima said. "What I'm talking about is a period of time where this person is cast outside the bounds of the community—not caged, just relocated—until both internal developmental progress and external developmental restitution are made.

"So if you take somebody's life, you should be responsible for filling that void," he continued. "If that person provided for a family, you are now responsible for providing for that family."

It made so much sense it almost made me mad. Not because I hadn't tripped him up, but because in explaining a system that diverts from the present one, Heshima revealed some maddening truths about America's criminal legal system I hadn't even thought of.

The breadwinner of a family is killed. Are garnished wages from someone making pennies doing prison labor going to actually support the family left behind? Absurd. My own conditioning had reared its head: I hadn't even thought about the element of redemption.

"I believe everyone can make a mistake, but no one should be barred from the capacity to change," Heshima said. "It's the only constant in nature: things either grow or they die."

Autonomous Infrastructure Mission proposes abandoning the current system and creating a new society perhaps geographically within its bounds but wholly independent of it. AIM accomplishes this through closed-circuit economics, seen in communities like Black Wall Street, but moreover through redefining education, safety, and community.

Perhaps it's easier for Heshima to abandon the current system because it has abandoned him. While California does not have explicit civil death laws—legal language that recognizes prisoners as having the same rights as a dead person—it might as well. Heshima's mail is constantly confiscated and his possession of certain books has been met with disciplinary citations. ~~First Amendment: freedom of speech.~~ His cell is tossed on a regular basis, his communications are screened by the mail staff, and his telephone calls are monitored. ~~Fourth Amendment: right to privacy.~~ In 2022 the US Supreme Court made a series of rulings that denied prisoners due process, gutting their ability to present evidence they were not adequately represented (*Shinn v. Ramirez*, 596 US ___, decided May 23, 2022) and their right to provide proof of their innocence (*Jones v. Hendrix*, 599 US ___, decided June 22, 2022). ~~Fifth Amendment: right to due process and fair procedures. Fourteenth Amendment: equal protection under the law.~~ In total, Heshima spent eighteen years and eight months in solitary confinement. ~~Eighth Amendment: cruel and unusual punishment.~~

"If they was to let me out today on parole, they could pull me over, search my car, come to my house in the middle of the night, pull me outta my bed, flip my mattress over, strip search me . . . and there wouldn't be anything I could do about it, because I'm not a person. I'm still J38283," Heshima said, referring to his prisoner ID. "That makes sense in this society, where if I was a ruling class element, or I was one of their tools like law enforcement and I was tasked with ensuring the continuation of this way of life, the guys whom I would make sure to keep my boot on they neck or my hand on they shoulder would be the guys who have very little interest in the continuation of such a system."

I imagined Heshima sitting in solitary, enclosed by concrete, with the dim glow of the hallway halogens seeping through the cracks of his food slot. Between his rights being stripped away and the darkness of Pelican Bay's solitary unit, it must have felt like an actual tomb. How was it that, so detached from society, he was able to envision a way to build a new one?

"I don't think it's hard for him to imagine," Duvon said. "The steps of AIM are very similar to how we grew up: Our mom planted a garden every year, had us eat cracked wheat with butter and salt for breakfast, fed our neighbors. Our dad taught us not to get trapped in the bad things that happen to you, to move on, to share your knowledge with the person who's coming up behind you."

For Heshima, the separation allowed him the time and space to perform a "concrete analysis of concrete conditions," a phrase coined by Mao and embraced by the Black Panther Party. It is the Marxist theory of dialectical materialism, which views historical and political events as the result of a series of contradictions or social conflicts.[18] With the world outside prison frozen in time, Heshima is able to examine these moments of conflict and contradiction, analyzing not the world he cannot access, but the history he can.

"The origin of our resistance lies in the very nature of the core contradictions of capitalist society in conflict with the advanced elements of its most oppressed strata: the bourgeois state's attempt to stamp out revolutionary sentiment amongst the lumpen-proletariat in hopes of maintaining and expanding its reactionary character," Heshima wrote in the *Bay View*. "[This is] in contrast with the struggle of political and politicized prisoners to raise the consciousness and revolutionary character of the entire underclass, all while resisting the fascist state's attempts to silence our dissent, crush our will to struggle and foment defection."[19]

(Told you he's prolific.)

The World Right Now by Scotty Scott aka Scott W. Smith

Conclusion:
Beyond Freedom

Oftentimes freedom is so elusive that just having a taste of it becomes a goal unto itself. But without a sure path forward, history has taught us, new systems often imitate the ones they replaced.

I was talking to a friend of mine from Egypt, who attended Cairo University during the Egyptian revolution of 2011. Buoyed by the eruption of the Arab Spring less than a year before, citizens across Egypt flooded the streets with flags, banners, and posters, banding together to withstand an intense military retaliation. For the majority of President Hosni Mubarak's thirty-year authoritarian rule, the people suffered economic hardship and brutal campaigns by the country's armed forces. Their thirst for freedom kept them on the streets for eighteen days until Mubarak resigned from his position, giving power over to the Supreme Council of the Armed Forces.

It was a massive undertaking, requiring the unprecedented mobilization of Egyptians from all socioeconomic backgrounds and costing the lives of 846 civilians.[1] Their unlikely success had benefits and drawbacks: They had found freedom, but it had been theoretical for so long, and no one had planned beyond grasping it.

This vacuum left in the aftermath of the revolution allowed room for the military to step in under the guise of maintaining order while the country found its footing. Boosted by its newfound power and influence, forces eventually mounted a military coup against the first democratically elected president, Mohamed Morsi. Subsequent clashes between the military and pro-Morsi protestors led to hundreds more civilian deaths. The military's political and economic stronghold on the state ultimately led to a return to authoritarianism. Abdel Fattah el-Sisi, the former minister of defense who led the military coup against Morsi, has defined his presidency by repressing public dissent—including forceful crackdowns on protests and freedom of the press—and economic policies that have led to extreme poverty; an estimated 20 million Egyptians are living at or below the poverty line.[2]

The Egyptian revolution can inform the current movement for liberation in the US in several ways. First and foremost, it proves revolution is possible. But it also provides a warning: *Freedom is not an end in itself.*

This volume has examined several evolutions of slavery—the prison-industrial complex, felony disenfranchisement, mass incarceration, economic disparities, redlining, and community destabilization. True freedom requires an account of all of these and a plan to ensure future evolutions do not occur.

"A new civil rights movement cannot be organized around the relics of the earlier system of control if it is to address meaningfully the racial realities of our time," Michelle Alexander writes in *The New Jim Crow*. "Any racial justice movement, to be successful, must vigorously challenge the public consensus that underlies the prevailing system of control."[3]

So hit the streets, organize mass protests, and make your voices heard. But attach yourself to a plan for the future, lest someone else plans it for you.

Brace Yourselves

The current landscape for activism is not for the faint of heart. This year police are on track to kill more people than any other year in the last decade. It doesn't even matter which year you're reading this. Fatal police shootings have increased annually since 2019.

There is also a well-organized counteroffensive already in full gear. The FBI is known to have used COINTELPRO tactics as recently as 2020, when the agency recruited an informant to infiltrate Black Lives Matter protests in Denver.[4] These active campaigns to undermine the integrity of racial justice movements are being deployed before the movement has a chance to fully heal from the damage of the last infiltration efforts, which led to the assassinations of Malcolm X, Fred Hampton, and Dr. Martin Luther King Jr. These wounds can be felt in the forms of constant in-fighting and divisive rhetoric meant to keep BIPOC (Black, Indigenous, and people of color) groups from banding together in a unified stand against white supremacy. They've also infected racial justice movements with *horizontal prejudice*, a term that acknowledges how individuals in a targeted racial group actually reinforce oppressive and discriminatory systems.

To be in the struggle for racial justice often feels Sisyphean. Endurance to press on in the face of ignorance and slow-turning wheels of justice and democracy seems impossible to maintain, but it is not. At the Shabazz Center's fifty-eighth commemoration of Malcolm X's death, Angela Davis said, "How is it possible to remain committed over so many centuries, over so many generations, to this struggle for freedom? That is phenomenal, that each generation has passed on that impulse to fight for freedom to the next."[5]

Fear not. As Davis stated, generations of experience are available to guide you through the labyrinth of obstacles that lay ahead. Through conversations with members of those generations, as well as my own experience, I've compiled four strategies to maintain your footing on this rugged path toward progress.

No. 1: Let the Movement Carry You

When I started working with All of Us or None, the first thing Dorsey said was, "This party started long before you walked in." Many of us come in on fire for our own ideas, but we neglect to acknowledge the vacuum within which those ideas were created. Likely, they were designed without the context of what has and hasn't worked in the past, nor an advanced understanding of how oppressive systems function and evolve—a knowledge gained only through dedicated trudging and ongoing political education. Like the students who met with Ivan Kilgore, carrying a cursory understanding and a backpack of buzzwords will not fare well in this fight.

As previously mentioned, the movements for equality and Black liberation have been trudging along for centuries. This can be seen as discouraging: People find it more comfortable to adapt to the status quo rather than fight long-standing, cunning systems of oppression that have, for the most part, prevailed over more just causes and movements. I urge you to see it otherwise.

An object in motion tends to stay in motion. As momentum carries the movement from generation to generation, so too are generations carried by the movement itself. Some of my dearest friends are those I formed connections with doing grassroots activism. We are like-minded, persistent, and always on the move. In each other, we find love, healing, and strength. It may sound cheesy, but amid an endless struggle, these acknowledgments of each other's humanity are essential to survival.

As George Jackson once wrote, "We can only be repressed if we stop thinking and stop fighting. People who refuse to stop fighting can never be repressed—they either win or they die—which is more attractive than losing and dying."[6]

Your final destination may not be clear, but if we're all on the road together, we can never end up lost. The road *will* lead somewhere, and when you arrive you will not be alone.

No. 2: Find Your Lane (And Stay in It)

In his critically acclaimed bestseller *Sapiens*, Yuval Noah Harari makes the argument that humans have conquered the world, reining in famine, plague, and war. His proof is in the number of people who die from obesity outpacing those who die from starvation; the number of people who die from old age eclipsing those who die from infectious diseases; and suicides beating out war casualties. I'm not sure I'd classify that last one as a win, but according to Harari, we did it. It's all rainbows and unicorns from here on out!

Back in reality, this world's got lots of problems. I remember reading *Sapiens* and finding it very difficult to get past the premise that we're ready to dismiss our failings and move on to the next phase of development. There are fights yet to be made for trans rights, reproductive rights, prison abolition, immigrant rights, labor unions, climate change, economic justice, racial justice, and countless others. It is possible to link several of these together via underlying oppressive structures, but too often the ecosystem of progressive organizations tries to take on everything at once in the hopes of arriving at Harari's utopia. Dismantling any single pain point requires laser focus, and the desire to do good in every vertical where evil exists can lead to muddy messaging and burnout.

If you have the energy for it, great. But this work will require endurance, and where you spend your energy and where you conserve it are important considerations. I maintain my endurance by dedicating my time to verticals linked by white supremacy—namely fights against antisemitism, racism, and criminal justice—by researching, interviewing, and exposing undeniable injustices and amplifying alternative structures. For vetted organizations in the fields of immigration reform, women's rights, and environmental justice, my support is more financial. I still participate, but not in a way that detracts from the causes I am more knowledgeable about and that require my full attention if I am serious about seeing them succeed.

So decide what you're most passionate about, how your skills are best suited to contribute, and remain focused.

No. 3: Avoid the Oppression Olympics

I bonded with Ken, my All of Us or None comrade who introduced me to revolutionary thinking, over our ancestors' shared traumas, but we could have just as easily been divided by it. We could have argued about whether or not the Holocaust was as horrific as slavery, or even about the validity of comparing the two. Instead we united in our pain, rather than presuming to understand the other's.

The term *Oppression Olympics* was coined by Chicana feminist Elizabeth Martínez in a conversation with Angela Davis at the University of California, San Diego in 1993.[7] In reflecting on this conversation years later, Davis would write in the foreword for Martínez's book that Martínez "urges us not to engage in 'Oppression Olympics' [or create] a futile hierarchy of suffering, but, rather, to harness our rage at persisting injustices to strengthen our opposition to an increasingly complex system of domination, which weaves together racism, patriarchy, homophobia, and global capitalist exploitation."[8]

Like any Olympic sport, the Oppression Olympics can be draining and exhausting. It requires energy that's better used to fight a common oppressor than each other. It is also a common tool of purveyors of oppressive systems, ensuring the fight is always among those vying for power, not against those who are *in* power.

When we first started organizing the Stop Killing Us rally at All of Us or None, a rash of infighting quickly spread between the Black and Latino members of the staff. Especially in a place like California, where Latinos are the largest racial and ethnic group at 39 percent of the population,[9] the number of Latino victims of police homicide also exceeded other races. The local and national trend, the Black contingency argued, was that *per capita* more Black individuals were killed by police, not to mention the fact that the murders igniting protests around the country were reactions to the deaths of two Black individuals (George Floyd and Breonna Taylor). Meeting after meeting, we debated over how many dead people from each race should be displayed on the posters I was charged with creating. In fact, the organization spent so much time fighting over the numbers that other elements of the protest—such as public outreach, media outreach, transportation, and more—were overlooked or rushed at the last minute. In the end, the posters displayed the per capita rate, but few victims of either race were given the attention they deserved: The protest was poorly attended, poorly covered by the media, and had little impact as a result.

In an effort to ease tensions, elders in the organization offered a way to approach intersectional situations without engaging in hierarchical suffering. Dorsey, for example, had participated in the 2006 protests against HR 4437, a federal legislation that would increase penalties for undocumented immigrants and classify them and anyone who helped them enter the country as felons. Many of the immigrants at risk were Haitian, but the vast majority were South American. According to Dorsey, the protestors presented a unified front—the most likely to succeed—by putting South American immigrants front and center. These individuals would then be responsible for acknowledging the far-reaching implications of the legislation, including the criminalization of their Haitian counterparts. Some states did end up passing similar legislation, but HR 4437 was defeated.

Focusing on suffering, or attempting to "out-suffer" another person, detracts from the focus required to end such suffering. Remind yourself that infighting is often the result of clandestine efforts by the ruling class to retain power by convincing those without power to participate in their own oppression, whether it be the FBI's counterintelligence program or the prison department's censorship of a ceasefire letter. Be clear of what you're fighting for and who you're fighting against.

No. 4: Laugh Out Loud

I was moderating a panel at Stony Brook University called Writing for Liberation when a graduate student raised her hand and asked about self-care.

"I can see how intense this is," she said after I had patched Ivan into the conference and the "this phone call and your telephone number may be recorded" memo had interrupted at least 100 times. Even in a conversation about liberation, the carceral system was managing to get a word in. "How and when do you find the space to breathe, to pause?"

It's a common question that many organizations are still grappling with. Some have healing retreats, where they shut down operations for a few days and meet with spiritual advisors. Others offer unlimited personal days or workshops around meditation and regeneration.

In my interviews for this book, I have found that elders in the movement have tremendous laughs. Woods laughs with their entire body. Ivan howls, and the harder he laughs, the higher his pitch becomes, working his way to a screeching cackle. With every "ha ha!" these tireless defenders of freedom produce massive exhales, expelling bodily toxins and opening up their lungs to large breaths of fresh air.

Ivan or Woods may not consciously see laughter as self-care, but I have found it to be a commonality among the toughest fighters in this space. Laughter is a kind of freedom that can't be chained or minimized, even by the most composed individuals or by the most repressive systems. In the words of Mark Twain, "Power, money, persuasion, supplication, persecution—these can lift at a colossal humbug—push it a little—weaken it a little, century by century, but only laughter can blow it to rags and atoms at a blast. Against the assault of Laughter nothing can stand."[10]

Maybe your own self-care isn't allowing yourself an uninhibited guffaw. But find a freedom that cannot be taken from you, and lean in.

Alternatives

I prefaced this book as an exploration of humanity. If nothing else, you've met some incredible humans. Perhaps you've been inspired to join them. Maybe you're intrigued but not convinced. Maybe their ideas have sparked some new ones within you. The more barriers to freedom the US's systems of law enforcement, punishment, and economics put on oppressed communities, the more limitless the freedom movement becomes. That includes its access points to newcomers and its opportunities to evolve.

"Because there are multiple ways in which the prison industrial complex infiltrates and impacts people's lives, there are multiple ways 1) to bring people to prison industrial complex abolition, and 2) to fight back," Woods explained. "Understanding that—as new people feel compelled by this politic—opens up new opportunities, not just in terms of capacity but also new opportunities for sites of struggle."

In that vein, I offer the following alternative organizations with which you may engage, although know there are many more.

The Movement for Black Lives

I would be remiss not to mention the Movement for Black Lives (https://m4bl.org), the governing organization of Black Lives Matter. Black Lives Matter is arguably the largest racial justice movement in modern history, with local chapters all over the country and several international chapters. Since its inception in 2012 following the killing of Trayvon Martin, the group has raised over $100 million in private funding and galvanized a new generation of activists. Their demonstrations have helped initiate federal oversight of police forces in Ferguson, Louisville, Baltimore, and Minneapolis. The Movement for Black Lives Electoral Justice project drafted a federal omnibus bill known as the BREATHE Act. Championed by Representatives Ayanna Pressley and Rashida Tlaib, the legislation calls for a reallocation of federal resources from law enforcement to community programs. It also proposes repealing the 1994 crime bill and the federal Three Strikes law.

A whole chapter can be written about the Movement for Black Lives, but the reason one is omitted here is simple: They didn't want me to write one.

I initially contacted the Movement for Black Lives in 2021 through its PR team. After two screening interviews about my project, I was granted a thirty-minute Zoom call with the organization's national field director and its director of partnerships. There was mistrust from the beginning—this was the first of many instances where I was asked "why" due to my skin tone—and both directors indicated that their willingness to participate in these kinds of relationships had been taken advantage of in the past. The downside of having a movement born and raised on the internet is that social media offers a chance for the widescale spread of disinformation. In fact, a month after my conversation with the Movement for Black Lives directors, the *New York Post* ran an unsubstantiated story based on a Facebook post that claimed one of its founders used BLM donations to purchase luxury houses.[II]

Perhaps more significantly, the Movement for Black Lives has ballooned into a robust apparatus of funding and resources, creating an abundance of ways its leaders can tell their stories without a conduit.

I'm not here to co-opt anyone's story, so if you're interested in the Movement for Black Lives or Black Lives Matter, its founders Patrisse Cullors, Alicia Garza, and Ayọ (formerly Opal) Tometi have written extensively and brilliantly about it. *When They Call You a Terrorist: A Black Lives Matter Memoir* by Patrisse Cullors and asha bandele and *The Purpose of Power: How We Come Together When We Fall Apart* by Alicia Garza both provide excellent tools for movement builders and organizers. You can also visit M4BL.org to learn about any one of their several campaigns and subprojects.

BYP100

Millennials' engagement in political and social movements has increased dramatically in the last five years. Between 2016 and 2018, there was a 10 percent increase in both political engagement and organized demonstrations among the members of this generation. More than 10,000 young people demonstrated against racial injustice after the police killings of George Floyd and Breonna Taylor in 2020, per data collected by the Brennan Center for Justice, leading to record civic engagement in the general election that year (half of the eligible voters aged eighteen to twenty-nine participated, compared with 39 percent in 2016).[12]

It should come as no surprise that a coalition of young activists arose from this surge of enthusiastic youth. Black Youth Project 100, or BYP100 (www.byp100.org), is a member-based organization of Black eighteen- to thirty-five-year-olds dedicated to creating justice and freedom for all Black people. Since the majority of its members are young and new to the movement, BYP100 conducts several educational workshops on grassroots organizing, fundraising, public policy debate, and electoral organizing.

With the guidance of American political scientist Dr. Cathy Cohen, the group defines its politic through a Black, queer, feminist lens, informed by the traditions of radical Black organizations such as the Student Nonviolent Coordinating Committee and the Combahee River Collective.

"It's not just about: 'We need to talk about women, we need to talk about queer folks, we need to talk about trans folks,'" BYP100 founder Charlene Carruthers told *The Root*. "We need to look to their work—historically and currently—because it puts us in a position to tell more complete stories. And when we tell more complete stories, we're able to craft more complete solutions."[13]

8toAbolition

When "Defund the Police" started to become trendy in the summer of 2020, many activists attempted to appease the majority of potential allies who may feel threatened by such a radical stance. They were quick to clarify that this demand was simply meant as a call for reallocation, not a call for abolition. They explained that the goal was to take surplus funds out of inflated police department budgets—funds designated, as an example, for military-grade equipment—and begin investing them in communities. It was something more digestible for the general public.

One of the leading coalitions for this strategy was Campaign Zero, which launched 8 Can't Wait (www.8cantwait.org), a campaign to implement certain reforms within police forces to curb police violence. Hard-liner abolitionists were appalled. The campaign had all the elements they despised: "reform," "police," and "wait." Within weeks a new coalition was born through internet chatter among some of these purists. They designed 8toAbolition (www.8toabolition.com), a direct response to 8 Can't Wait, and when they say defund the police, they mean what you think they mean: the eradication of police and prisons.

The authors of 8toAbolition—Mon Mohapatra, Leila Raven, Nnennaya Amuchie, Reina Sultan, K Agbebiyi, Sarah T. Hamid, Micah Herskind, Derecka Purnell, Eli Dru, and Rachel Kuo—are a diversified group of individuals spread across the country. They are, in no particular order, Black, Latino, Asian, Arab, Muslim, white, trans, queer, migrant, disabled, sex working, caregiving, and working-class. And while their identities vary greatly, their identity politics are closely aligned. Put simply, that politic boils down to this: "We believe in a world where there are zero police murders because there are zero police."

Together the group members envisioned an eight-point path to justice, as outlined on the organization's website, 8toabolition.com:

- **Defund the police** by enacting the highest budget cuts each year until the budget is zero.

- **Demilitarize communities** by ending police militarization programs and repealing policies like broken-windows policing and hot-spot policing.

- **Remove police from schools** and prohibit surveillance of Black and Brown students by school officials through programs that criminalize them.

- **Free people from jails and prisons** and reject all "alternatives to incarceration," including electronic monitoring and coercive programs.

- **Repeal laws that criminalize survival,** such as homelessness, sex work, and mandatory arrests in domestic violence cases.

- **Invest in community self-governance** by promoting neighborhood councils and funding community-based public safety approaches such as non-carceral violence prevention and intervention programs.

- **Provide housing for everyone** by repurposing empty buildings, houses, apartments, and hotels.

- **Invest in care, not cops**, by redirecting funds allocated for law enforcement to programs that build community relationships and resources for mutual aid and transformative responses to harm.

The preceding is a simplification of the organization's very detailed plan for a better future. If you're interested in the mission to build a society that transfers safety and well-being from police to communities, 8toAbolition has several resources that detail specific demands, as well as tools for amplification on social media.

The Alliance for Safety and Justice

If the chapters regarding mass incarceration piqued your interest, you'll want to acquaint yourself with the Alliance for Safety and Justice. Many organizations are fighting mass incarceration by way of research-based advocacy—the Sentencing Project, the Marshall Project, and Prison Policy Initiative, just to name a few—but the Alliance for Safety and Justice stands out because it is driven by directly impacted individuals with *inside* knowledge . . . literally.

For the last four years, the organization has been led by CEO Jay Jordan, founder and poster child of the ongoing #TimeDone campaign. Jordan organizes individuals like himself who are living with conviction histories and face countless barriers to success long after their sentence has expired. The campaign took on California's Ban the Box movement, which ultimately removed the requirement for job applicants to disclose their criminal history. Testifying about his struggles with stigma and unemployment after incarceration, Jordan

has worked with many organizations, both as a staffer and a participant in several coalitions, to create more accessible options for equity
and personal development for those leaving prison.[14]

In addition to incorporating the #TimeDone campaign, the Alliance for Safety and Justice brings the victims of crime into the conversation regarding imprisonment and punishment. For example, in 2022,
the organization surveyed more than 80,000 crime survivors from
across the country to gauge their views on public safety. The resulting
report, *Crime Survivors Speak: National Survey of Victims' Views on Safety
and Justice*, had several revelatory findings, such as less than 50 percent
are allowed conferences with the perpetrator upon conviction, and 68
percent said they would rather see taxpayer dollars invested in crime
prevention, crisis assistance, and strong communities than increases
in arrests, longer sentences, and incarceration.[15]

I worked with Jay, who stepped down from his role at ASJ in late
2023, on Proposition 17, the California ballot measure to end felony
disenfranchisement in the state. (We won.) When he speaks he commands the room, so I'll let him leave a final thought, this one from his
appearance on *The Problem with Jon Stewart*:

"We don't have a public safety system in this country. We have a
crime response system."[16]

Choose Your Own Liberation

The racial and economic divides in America are man-made and
deeply rooted in the nation's identity. The latter makes the struggle to
close the gaps painfully challenging, but the former ensures its prob-
ability. If people can create a divide, they can build a bridge to cross it.

We have been conditioned to believe that those people are our
elected representatives, when in reality politicians would more readily save themselves, and their positions of power, than anything
else. You have to wonder about the kind of person who would run
for political office. They're ambitious. They're willing to bend their
values to appease voters. They're seemingly willing to undermine

their constituents only to later engage them in futile collaborative endeavors.

This is not a political book, because I have long given up on political solutions. Proposed and enacted by people who strive for individual power rather than collective power, legislative actions have never gone far enough when it comes to real change. Legislation is entangled in a system of legal precedent and social control, and it falls prey to rollbacks, caveats, carve-outs, and reversals. More commonly, they serve as rhetorical tools to push party-lines agendas, with both Democrats and Republicans more interested in maintaining a majority in a finite chamber of members, rather than what is good for the majority of their constituents.

After the 2020 general election, I changed my voter registration to No Party. This angered many of my liberal friends, who interpreted my decision as indifference. In some respects, they were correct, but not entirely.

I remember the moment I made my pivot quite clearly: I was at Outback Steakhouse, nervously cramming Bloomin' Onion bits into my mouth while watching the Super Tuesday primary numbers come in on the TV behind the bar. The race had come down to Joe Biden and Bernie Sanders, and I was pulling for Bernie. Yes, he was another old white man, but so was the other guy. I liked Bernie because he hated fanfare. Rather than a stage with intro music and waving American flags, Bernie announced his first candidacy in 2016 by walking outside his office, telling a handful of reporters he was running for president, and then walking away to finish his lunch break. I liked that he was about the work, not about the performance art that has come to plague each congressional hearing and presidential debate. In politics there is always drama, because when there isn't, people don't pay attention.

The drama in the 2016 and 2020 primaries came at the expense of the most unwilling participant: my boy Bernie. In 2016 WikiLeaks exposed emails between top officials of the Democratic National Committee mocking Bernie and vowing to undermine his campaign. As I sat munching on fried onions, I watched another successful campaign for the establishment. The day before, three major candidates—Pete Buttigieg, Tom Steyer, and Amy Klobuchar—withdrew, each endorsing Joe Biden. In fact, every major candidate who had bowed out before Super Tuesday—Beto O'Rourke, Kamala Harris, Cory Booker, Julián Castro, Andrew Yang, and Michael Bloomberg—had endorsed Joe. For the casual primary voter, their party was telling them only one candidate made sense. I had just asked for more dipping sauce when CNN made its projections: 629 pledged delegates for Joe, 539 for Bernie. A month later, Bernie dropped out.

Change is hard. None of us really like it—even when we yearn for it—and politicians *hate* it. Bernie had proposed changes that appeared radical in 2016, things like Medicare for all, the Green New Deal, and free college tuition. Even though all of these were mainstream talking points by 2020—free college tuition morphed into the debate over student loan forgiveness—Bernie was ostracized by the Democratic Party in the name of maintaining the status quo. The primaries, like most politics, had simply become a game, and I was done playing.

The truth is, stripped down of all rhetoric, America's two parties are divided on two talking points, and two talking points alone: guns and abortion. Everything outside those subjects is hot air, the passion behind it fueled solely by the desire to maintain power. The parties are so alike that they've been able to swap titles, with Southern Democrats becoming Republicans and more liberal voters becoming Democrats in 1964, a period known as "realignment."

I still engage in politics, particularly when it comes to local elections, for two reasons. The first is the suffering I've seen in the eyes and body language of those who have been stripped of their right to vote. In my many interviews researching articles about felony disenfranchisement, I've heard about the pains of feeling like a "non-person," of having no say in the decisions that impact your life, of desperately attempting to reintegrate into society, while constantly being reminded that you still cannot really be a part of it. I vote for the people who cannot.

The second reason is more of a long game. The other day, my son fell off his scooter and scraped his knee. I think the sight of gushing blood streaming down his leg hurt more than the wound itself, and it certainly scared the shit out of me. My instinct as his mother, however, isn't to walk away and hope he finds his way to a doctor who can fix him. No, I clean the wound, put a bandage on it, and get him an ice pack. I do what I can to curb the bleeding until we can get to an urgent care. That's how I feel about voting. The options are never ideal and, at best, inadequate to fix the problem, but I'll do what I can until a more viable option becomes available.

The longest-running ideological shortcoming seems to be this idea of there not being enough for everyone: not enough money, not enough housing, not enough food, not enough freedom. Even the most staunch advocates for Adam Smith's capitalism seem to have lost touch with his original hypothesis: That society is not composed of a zero-sum, finite-pie amount of substance, where one person's gain means another's loss. The thought of freedom should not be threatening to anyone, and a *true* patriot would embrace the struggle to achieve it.

Some may read this book and think, "What does she know about patriotism? She clearly hates America!" I get it. And when I first started writing this book, I might have agreed with them. I had stopped singing the national anthem at sporting events, and I hated the Fourth of July. The fireworks scared my dogs, woke up the baby, and in celebration of what? What was there left to love in a society so entrenched in divisive rhetoric and oppressive systems?

What I learned through the process of writing this book, however, is that the individuals I talked to really love the people of this country and believe in the promise of democracy and freedom, although yet unfulfilled. It's still all about survival, but collective survival, collective uplift. They believe in people and their ability to self-liberate, collaborate, share responsibility, and care for each other. That belief is what I've come to embrace as American.

You can tell the story of this country two ways. The first is a story of atrocities. That story begins with the genocide of the people who called this land home long before it was discovered by Europeans, climaxes with the kidnapping and enslavement of Africans, and culminates with 2,000 Black men and women killed by police in a five-year span.

The second is a story of revolution. Of people who fought together in Bacon's Rebellion. People who fought together against the British, the only colors of division being the ones dyed into their frock coats. It's the story of people who were hosed down, hounded by hounds, and who returned to the streets the next day to fight again. It's the story of a well-trodden Edmund Pettus Bridge, crossed on Bloody Sunday (March 7, 1965) when state troopers attacked unarmed, peaceful marchers with billy clubs and tear gas; crossed again in 2015 by members of local Black churches who walked the bridge starting from the Montgomery side—what they termed as a "reverse march"— protesting new rollbacks to the Civil Rights Act; crossed the next day when then-President Barack Obama and Rep. John Lewis led another group along the same path to commemorate the fiftieth anniversary of the initial crossing; crossed again in July 2020 as a horse-drawn wagon carried Lewis's casket over the expanse. Back and forth, back and forth, each footfall a determined step in the direction of freedom, justice, and equality.

Neither story has an ending, nor are they independent of each other. But you get to decide which story you want to be a part of. You can contribute to the nation's atrocities, or you can participate in revolutionary change that embodies the freedom it presumes to uphold. There is no middle ground: Abstaining is simply opting to engage in the former by default.

Should you choose the growing movement of liberation, be as systematic about dismantling the nation's defects as its early citizens were about embedding them in its fabric. Learn about history, not as a way of focusing on the past but as a way of informing you, the way the individuals profiled in this book have been informed by their own histories. Our collective experience will provide tools to aid in our collective salvation.

You have individual tools as well: a prominent social media account, perhaps, or a knack for storytelling. Maybe you have surplus food, surplus land, that can be developed into community resources. Maybe you have money to fund programs created by incarcerated activists. Add your individual tools to the larger box of collective tools, and apply them to a plan. Take the lessons learned from the past, and forge a path forward. Pave a wide road that can accommodate everyone who's willing to help propel the movement in the direction of freedom. And when you arrive, build a foundation strong enough to last.

Glossary

ACCOUNTABILITY   Refers to how people hold themselves to a set of community standards and responsibility. Accountability requires any violator of those standards or responsibilities to be present and confronted with a complete examination of the impact of their action. Accountability can be imposed by an external institution, such as a court or organization, but it can also be applied internally through a process of reflection, whether spiritual, faith-based, or otherwise.

ALLY   An ally works externally to support and amplify the struggles of oppressed groups. Internally, they commit to recognizing and examining their own privilege—be it racially based or stemming from a gender or class difference—while committing to reducing their own footprint in the system of oppression that targets these groups. Allies operate with the understanding that oppression impacts every community, even if it's only directed at one group in particular.

ANTISEMITISM   A hatred or fear of Jews, Judaism, Jewish culture, and related symbols, either by disparagement or generic bias.

ASSIMILATION   In anthropological and sociological settings, assimilation is the absorption of individuals of colonized cultures and heritages into the mainstream. Colloquially, it is embodied in the "love it or leave it" rebuke to critics of the status quo. After then-President Donald Trump resurfaced this rhetoric in 2018, Ibram X. Kendi, author of *How to Be an Antiracist*, told *Mother Jones,* "My initial thought is that it sort of conveys—particularly to people of color—that this is not our home."[1]

BAN THE BOX   Ban the Box refers to state and national campaigns for fair chance employment, specifically by removing questions from initial job application forms that reference criminal history. In some states, checks for crimes relating to the employer's specific industry may be conducted after a full assessment of the applicant's qualifications. Nearly 77 million Americans are impacted by the stigma of incarceration when it comes to finding employment after serving their sentence.[2] Ban the Box advocates point to research-based evidence that employment reduces recidivism rates among people coming out of incarceration. Furthermore, their participation in business and gainful employment betters the economy.

BLACK FEMINISM   Black feminism grew out of the intersection of anti-racism and anti-sexism. The Combahee River Collective, a group of Black feminists formed in the 1970s, defined their politic as such: "Black women are inherently valuable, that [Black women's] liberation is a necessity not as an adjunct to somebody else's but because of our need as human persons for autonomy."[3]

BLACK LIVES MATTER (CONCEPT)   The ideology that unequivocally condemns police violence against and homicides of Black people by police. This is not to the exclusion of violence against people of other races. Rather, it is deployed as a method of highlighting the systematic inequalities Black people face in various institutions and law enforcement policies.

BLACK PANTHER PARTY   A revolutionary organization formed in 1966, it served as a safety and social program, autonomous of the federal and state governments. In addition to embracing philosophies regarding arming oneself as a means of protection—as well as reparations and the release of Black prisoners—the Black Panther Party provided social programs such as free breakfasts for children and medical clinics.

CIVIL DISOBEDIENCE   A method of political protest embraced and deployed by civil rights leaders like Dr. Martin Luther King Jr. It espouses the use of nonviolent means to disobey laws that promote inequality.

COINTELPRO   Shorthand for Counterintelligence Program, COINTELPRO was a covert operation used by the FBI to discredit and neutralize groups the agency deemed to be "subversive" to US political stability. The program used infiltration and leverage to pressure, criminalize, and undermine movement leaders and foster infighting, often in violation of constitutional rights. These campaigns against leaders of the 1960s Black liberation movements led to the assassinations of Dr. Martin Luther King Jr., Malcolm X, and Fred Hampton. The program was officially active between 1956 and 1971, but reports of similar infiltration methods have been discovered as recently as 2020.

COLORBLIND RACISM   Explored in depth by Michelle Alexander in her seminal book *The New Jim Crow,* colorblind racism is a complex, almost inadvertent form of racism. It is espoused by people who presume to "not see" skin color or race in their daily interactions. Although the idea may generate from an authentic belief that all people should be treated equally regardless of their race or ethnicity, in practice it invalidates the value of peoples' culture and ignores centuries of racist policies that have created systematic discrepancies that put Black people at a disadvantage.

CRIMINALIZATION   A legislature-initiated act that deems certain behaviors illegal and punishable under law.

CULTURAL RACISM   The establishment of white people's behaviors and values as "the norm" or superior to the culture of other races. In a gross oversimplification, it is the indoctrination of a media-heavy society to believe in the validity of white supremacy through representations of white superheroes and Black villains. It can also manifest in magazines, television, and advertisements that define what is "beautiful," and news outlets that widely publish the plight of a white child while omitting coverage of similar or worse atrocities committed against children of color.

DEFUND THE POLICE   A way of addressing police violence that stops short of total abolition. It is based on a reallocation of funds to government agencies that are designed to bolster underserved communities, particularly in education, housing, and youth services. The funds proposed for reallocation range from decarceration-centered reforms to demilitarizing police agencies.

DIRECTLY IMPACTED   A term used by anti-carceral advocacy groups to refer to people with criminal histories—those directly impacted by the criminal justice system.

EQUITY   Equity requires both equal opportunity for advancement and the removal of barriers set in front of certain groups pursuing advancement. This desire for advancement is not solely financial. It is a desire to reach one's full potential and attain a quality of life for themselves and their family.

FREE SPEECH MOVEMENT   A series of demonstrations conducted by students at the University of California, Berkeley, during the 1964–65 school year. The movement was triggered by the suspension of students from two on-campus groups—the Congress for Racial Equality and the Student Nonviolent Coordinating Committee—for allegedly recruiting students for off-campus political actions. As many as 7,000 students demonstrated in solidarity with the organizers who were suspended and arrested for conducting political activity that included the proliferation of information regarding racial inequities and injustices throughout the country. The Free Speech Movement marked a new generation of student activists who would go on to participate in the civil rights movement and protest the war in Vietnam.

GPS MONITORING GPS monitors were first used in the 1960s after brothers at Harvard retrofitted old military equipment to create an anklet meant to monitor the movements of young defendants to ensure they showed up to court cases.[4] Over time the technology evolved from using radio signals to GPS locating and cell tower signals. Today the global industry for GPS tracking devices is estimated at $3.1 billion.[5]

GRASSROOTS MOVEMENTS Movements designed around mobilizing community members. They engage communities impacted by a particular oppressive system to deploy strategies designed by movement leaders to dismantle that system. At the heart of grassroots movement is self-liberation.

HBCUS Historically Black colleges and universities were developed in the 1960s to offer higher education to Black youth still being excluded from many educational institutions. There are 99 HBCUs between the US, the District of Columbia, and the US Virgin Islands. Non-Black students make up 25 percent of enrollment.[6]

HISTORICAL TRAUMA The multigenerational emotional and psychological repercussions of profound atrocities—such as slavery or forced relocation—on communities.

HORIZONTAL PREJUDICE A term that acknowledges how individuals from a targeted racial group actually reinforce discriminatory and oppressive systems.

HOT-SPOT POLICING   A method of identifying areas of high crime concentration through algorithms and flooding those areas with police officers. The most notorious use of hot-spot policing was the "stop-and-frisk" policy instituted by then-New York Mayor Michael Bloomberg.

INSTITUTIONAL RACISM   The result of policies and practices with a single agency that have produced racially divided results at a chronic level. Variations in outcomes for people of different races may be intentional or accidental, but they are consistent and deeply embedded in the institution's foundational elements. The government's segregation laws and denial of home loans to people living in areas with a Black resident majority (redlining) are both forms of institutional racism.

JIM CROW   Jim Crow refers to an era when laws criminalized Black life and enforced racial segregation. These laws, such as racially segregated public facilities and public vagrancy, were instituted primarily at the state level after the American Civil War, when Southern states sought a way to preserve free labor after a costly conflict. While many Jim Crow laws originated in the late nineteenth century, many remained in place until the 1960s.

LGBTQ   An acronym used to define one's sexual orientation. Its initials stand for lesbian, gay, bisexual, transgender, and queer or questioning. A recent evolution of the acronym includes the letters *I* and *A* as well as a plus sign (LGBTQIA+). *I* stands for intersex (a term for bodies that fall outside the male/female binary) and *A* for asexual or aromantic. The plus sign is an acknowledgment that the sexual orientation spectrum is still being explored and other expressions of sexuality may still be unknown.

MARGINALIZED   A term based on a visual representation of society as having a flush and concentrated center, with diminishing substance and resources farther from the middle. Being marginalized is being pushed to the outer edge of this design through exclusive policies and barriers to advancement.

MASS INCARCERATION The term highlights the United States utilizing criminalization as a method of large-scale racial and social control. It was first used as a way of differentiating the US from the rest of the world—both developed and underdeveloped countries—and how the US imprisons its population. It is also an acknowledgment of the 600 percent increase in prison population between the 1970s and 2000s due to America's War on Drugs.

MOVEMENT BUILDING Campaigns around social and racial justice are powered by movement building. Rather than doing demonstrative actions, movement builders focus on strengthening the foundation of groups vying for social change; they create connections between like-minded individuals and organizations and empower movements, either by providing resources or proliferating messaging and humanizing narratives. Ultimately, the goal is to build up a movement so it can effectively engage with power holders and garner public support for the visions of equity and justice.

PEOPLE OF COLOR A collective term for non-white racial groups. Not to be confused with the racist inference of "colored people," people of color is a way of unifying racial groups against white supremacy culture. A more modern version is BIPOC (Black, Indigenous, people of color), calling attention to the more severe consequences of systemic racism on Black and Indigenous communities.

POWER A relational way of describing one's influence over another. Power is particularly significant when it influences access and control over societal elements governing politics, education, and health care. That is not to say those without access are powerless. Rather, every group has power in its ability to either reinforce or disrupt relationships with institutions, systems, or assemblies it interacts with.

RACE   A social construct developed as a way to ensure people of different skin color in the same economic class did not unify against the ruling class. While we identify race primarily by variations in skin color, this idea of race as a social construction has allowed it to be applied to people of similar ancestral lineages, cultural histories, and ethnic backgrounds.

RACIAL JUSTICE   A movement rooted in racial equity and systemic shifts in power that rectify long-term discriminatory practices across an array of institutions and policies. Racial justice requires both eliminating outdated policies that deliberately or inadvertently produce unequal treatment of non-white communities, as well as introduce policies that proactively serve to support and sustain racial equity. The ideal of racial justice is a society that functions with systemic fairness and a level playing field from which individuals, regardless of race, can thrive.

RACIAL WEALTH GAP   A term to describe the lasting effects of discriminatory practices among a confluence of systems. Disparities in how non-white employees are treated by corporations, banks, educational institutions, and other key players on the road to financial gain have denied upward mobility. Although some individuals have successes, there is an absence of generational wealth—the ability of one generation to leave assets to the next—among marginalized communities. Black and Latino families are twice as likely as white families to have "zero wealth," meaning their debts are of matching value to their assets.

RECONSTRUCTION ERA   Referring to the years immediately following the Civil War, between 1865 and 1877. During this time the former Confederacy was folded back into the United States, which resulted in a number of compromises and carve-outs that Southern politicians insisted they needed for the South's ability to survive without slavery.

RESTORATIVE JUSTICE   Refers to an alternative method of accountability and reconciliation that is focused on healing. Restorative justice shifts power from the court to the people most directly harmed by the alleged actions. Methods often feature meetings between the perpetrator of a crime and their victim; through these meetings, instances of crime create opportunities for community building and victim satisfaction.

SCHOOL-TO-PRISON PIPELINE   A grim trend identified in the 1980s of minority students entering the juvenile justice system. The implementation—and present-day preservation—of "zero tolerance" introduced law enforcement to school premises and created criminal consequences for non-criminal offenses (things that may be reprehensible to a school administrator, but not seen as criminal in the eyes of the law). According to a report from the American Civil Liberties Union, African Americans accounted for 31 percent of school-related arrests.[7]

SOCIAL JUSTICE   A process by which commonly oppressed groups seek equal access to resources, opportunities, and seats of power. As a group forms, they challenge oppressive systems and empower its members by reinforcing autonomy, which reinforces solidarity.

STRUCTURAL/SYSTEMIC RACISM   The validation and legitimization of systems that have historically advantaged white citizens over their non-white counterparts. Systemic racism is manifested in America's policies, social fabric, and governing institutions as a method of reinforcing white supremacy over infinite generations. To that end, it is in a constant state of evolution, resurfacing old, pejorative practices in new, seemingly colorblind forms. It is a way of preserving institutional racism in ways that are perceived to be justified, thereby normalizing its existence and effect.

SURVEILLANCE　A vast system of technological tools used by police agencies to monitor the public with little oversight. Surveillance tools can include CCTV cameras, automatic license plate readers, and cell phone tracking devices.

SYSTEM IMPACTED　A term used by anti-carceral advocacy groups to refer to people affected by the criminal justice system but who have not been prosecuted or incarcerated. The most common system-impacted individual is one whose loved one is directly impacted.

THREE STRIKES LAW　A legal statute derived from baseball terminology. The Three Strikes law varies in application from state to state—it currently exists in twenty-eight states, as well as the federal criminal code—but essentially imposes mandatory long-term sentencing for defendants convicted of "serious felonies" three times.[8] To finish the terminology, they are "out" after three strikes, as many are sentenced to life in prison. The law has not proven to decrease crime.

Acknowledgments

When searching for a foreword writer, it was important to me to frame the book in a Black feminist lens. Throughout my writing journey, I had come to embrace this particular theory of change—partly because of my own experiences as a woman, but mostly because of the relationships I'd made—and was eager to infuse the foundation for *Reimagining the Revolution* with the sense of strength and determination I'd seen exemplified by Black women in this space. When Ilyasah Shabazz replied affirmatively, I literally fell out of my chair.

Ilyasah is an incredible human being, and I'm deeply honored and humbled to have her introduce my work. Not only does she do justice to the work of her mother, Dr. Betty Shabazz, and her father, Malcolm X, through her work at the Shabazz Center, she has carved out a space for herself as an individual with her own contributions to the work of racial justice and liberation. I am forever grateful for her grace in our interactions and for her invaluable contribution to this project.

Like many stories, mine began with a mother and a father, William and Sandra Lehman. And while I certainly "didn't come with instructions," as my mother likes to say, they supported my unconventional career path, read versions of my manuscript, offered feedback, and celebrated milestones. Thank you, Mom and Dad, for your support.

I started this project in quarantine with my husband, James, and my son, Isaac. We both had full-time jobs and it seemed absolutely insane to start writing a book. But James has always believed in me, long before I believed in myself. It is his unwavering faith and fantastic co-parenting skills that allowed me to make this dream a reality.

The first leap of faith was to start my career as an author, which, as a parent, seemed irresponsible. Undeterred, I launched a Kickstarter for the book. The backers of that project allowed me to pursue this full-time. A huge thanks to: Barry J. Schneider, Spencer Ferebee, Josh Lehman, Michelle Killmer, Francine Patterson, Nancy Levin, Sally Breckenridge, Sam Adams, Jenna Scalmanini, CT Turney-Lewis, Carol Schwartz, Ben Summers, Tom Adkins, Margot Edelman, Libby, Scott Ewing, Heather Yeager, Rachel Comerford, Clint and Rebecca Allen, Nadeen Reinecke, Riry Jones, Ciro Scotti, Kalene Kobs, Win Bennett, Billy Doyle, Sara O'Sullivan, AJ Snow, Francine Klein, Jordy Velasquez, Paige Midstokke, Samuel Salzinger, Doug Hills, Debra Schneider, Donald Lehman, Shane Nelson, Stephen Salisbury, Jeanne Mariani, Jacob Hartman, Marcie Burros, Susan Dreyfus, Abhishek Sheth, RJ Marshall, Riley Lehman, Fool's Moon Entertainment Inc., Basil Carr, Tiffany Seeler, Linda Latman, Cindy Opdyke, Jimmy D'Amico, Kathy Hendrickson, Lanny, Brittany, Sarah, Terry Schneider, Katie Greene, Han-Hui Ling, David Ettinger, Jack Fitzsimmons, Ali Wallick, Colin Chazen, Shelley Mendelsohn, Bookwyrmkim, Heath Shuford, Taube Kravitz, Travis Allen, Sarah Kalloch, Emmo Lütringer, Brent Sisson, Milton A. Early, John Szymanski, Allan Hoving, Jay Sherman, Kathleen Adkins, Nathan, Michael Roosevelt, Drew Raine, Jackson, Joyce Guse, Dani, Sebastien Tilmans, Sarah Smith, MYS, Michael Kazin, Katie Talwar, Heather Lehman, Hilary Rosen, Spencer Lawrence, JoAnne Hammes, Jeannette Spangler, Brian Bondurant, The Creative Fund by BackerKit, George D. Cochrane, and John Miyasato.

Three other individuals contributed to the Kickstarter: My loving and eternally gorgeous grandmother Audrey Schneider and my beautiful girls, Rebecca Lubart and Molly Schroeder. You are the women who lift me up and keep me afloat when the tides rise and fall.

I could not have written a word in this volume if it wasn't for the insight of Ken Oliver, who opened my mind to the world of revolution and challenged me to think differently about the world around me. He is a beacon of hope and an example of what can be achieved if you believe in yourself and never give up.

Thanks to my writing partner, Jason Masino, who Ubered all the way out to the burbs for lengthy writing sessions and went over several drafts. I also want to thank my sponsor, John, whose faith I've borrowed several times throughout this process.

A special thanks to Keith Donnell Jr. for assisting in the editing process as a sensitivity reader and, at times, calling me out on my own unintentional biases.

Finally, I want to acknowledge North Atlantic Books and my editor, Shayna Keyles, in particular, for bringing this book to the world. They took a chance on an unagented, debut author because they believed in the importance of and the need for these stories. I am eternally grateful for their commitment to bringing marginalized voices closer to rooms where real change can be affected.

Notes

Author's Note: About the Artists

1. Diane Khan, "Gerald Morgan, 25 Years Inside," Humans of San Quentin, n.d., https://humansofsanquentin.org/beyond-story/gerald-morgan -25-years-inside/.
2. Scott Smith, "COVID Creature," *All of Us or None*, September 2020, 4.
3. Scott Smith, "Why the Statue of Liberty Is an Imposter," Prison Journalism Project, May 2, 2023, https://prisonjournalismproject.org /2023/05/10/everyone-i-know-in-prison-poor/.

Preface

1. Paula Lehman-Ewing and Legal Services for Prisoners with Children, "Involuntary Servitude: Life as Civilly Dead," *All of Us or None*, June 2020.
2. "California Proposition 57, Parole for Non-Violent Criminals and Juvenile Court Trial Requirements (2016)," Ballotpedia, n.d., https:// ballotpedia.org/California_Proposition_57,_Parole_for_Non-Violent _Criminals_and_Juvenile_Court_Trial_Requirements_(2016).
3. Frantz Fanon, *Black Skin, White Masks* (Grove, 2008), xiv.
4. "Black Codes - Definition, Dates & Jim Crow Laws | HISTORY," HISTORY, June 1, 2010, https://www.history.com/topics/black-history /black-codes.
5. Christopher Uggen, Ryan Larson, Sarah Shannon, and Robert Stewart, "Locked Out 2022: Estimates of People Denied Voting Rights," Sentencing Project, November 23, 2022, www.sentencingproject.org/reports/locked -out-2022-estimates-of-people-denied-voting-rights/.

Chapter 1: The Way We Move

1   Michelle Alexander, *The New Jim Crow: Mass Incarceration in the Age of Colorblindness* (New Press, 2010), 180.

2   Dani Anguiano, "US Prison Workers Produce $11bn Worth of Goods and Services a Year for Pittance," *Guardian,* June 15, 2022, www.theguardian .com/us-news/2022/jun/15/us-prison-workers-low-wages-exploited.

3   Uggen et al., "Locked Out 2022."

4   Emily Widra and Tiana Herring, "States of Incarceration: The Global Context 2021," Prison Policy Initiative, September 2021, www.prisonpolicy .org/global/2021.html.

5   "Crime Survivors Speak: The First-Ever National Survey of Survivors of Crime," Alliance for Safety and Justice, 2022, https://allianceforsafety andjustice.org/wp-content/uploads/documents/Crime%20Survivors %20Speak%20Report.pdf.

6   Larry Buchanan, Quoctrung Bui, and Jugal Patel, "Black Lives Matter May Be the Largest Movement in U.S. History," *New York Times*, July 3, 2020, www.nytimes.com/interactive/2020/07/03/us/george-floyd-protests -crowd-size.html.

7   Mapping Police Violence website, n.d., https://mappingpoliceviolence.us/.

8   "Clark County, Nevada Covid Case and Risk Tracker," *New York Times*, April 1, 2021, www.nytimes.com/interactive/2021/us/clark-nevada-covid -cases.html.

9   Paula Lehman-Ewing, "Analysis of LA County Pretrial Risk Assessment Tools Raises Questions," *Los Angeles Daily Journal*, December 5, 2018.

10 Sam Reisman, "The Rise of the Progressive Prosecutor," Law360, April 7, 2019, www.law360.com/articles/1145615/the-rise-of-the-progressive -prosecutor.

11 Mapping Police Violence.

12 Catroiona Harvey-Jenner, "'Elizabeth from Knoxville' Goes Viral after Video Shows Rioter Complaining about Being Pepper Sprayed," *Cosmopolitan*, January 7, 2021.

13 Alexander, *New Jim Crow*, 235.

Chapter 2: Systems of Oppression

1   Dan Baum, "Legalize It All," *Harper's*, April 2016, https://harpers.org /archive/2016/04/legalize-it-all/.

2   George Jackson, *Blood in My Eye* (Black Classic Press, 1990), 183.

3   Brian Resnick, "Racist Anti-Immigrant Cartoons from the Turn of the 20th Century," *Atlantic*, November 27, 2014, www.theatlantic.com /national/archive/2011/11/racist-anti-immigrant-cartoons-from-the-turn -of-the-20th-century/383248/.

4   Henry Pratt Fairchild, *Greek Immigration to the United States* (Yale University Press, 1911).

5   Stefano Harney and Fred Moten, *The Undercommons: Fugitive Planning & Black Study* (Autonomedia, 2013), 42.

6   Richard Rothstein, *The Color of Law: A Forgotten History of How Our Government Segregated America* (Liveright, 2017), 5.

7   Rothstein, *Color of Law*, 50.

8   Rothstein, viii.

9   Ruth Wilson Gilmore, *Golden Gulag: Prisons, Surplus, Crisis, and Opposition in Globalizing California* (University of California Press, 2007), 90.

10 John Kelly, Soo Rin Kim, Meredith Deliso, Mark Nichols, and Grace Manthey, "How Much Do Police Officers Mirror the Communities They Serve? ABC News Looked at the Data," ABC News, May 20, 2021.

11 Sabrina Laverty, *Uncompetitive and Unrepresented: Voters Locked out of Representation*, FairVote, May 3, 2023, https://fairvote.org/report /uncompetitive-and-unrepresented-voters-locked-out-of-representation/.

12 Jonas Hanway, *Solitude in Imprisonment* (London, 1776).

13 John Locke, "An Essay Concerning Human Understanding," 1690.

14 Gilmore, *Golden Gulag*, 12.

15 April K. Cassou and Brian Taugher, "Determinate Sentencing in California: The New Numbers Game," *McGeorge Law Review* (University of the Pacific) 9, no. 1 (1978): 5–106, https://scholarlycommons.pacific.edu/mlr /vol9/iss1/8/.

16 *Jones v. Hendrix*, 599 US ___.

17 Gilmore, *Golden Gulag*, 14.

18 The Times Editorial Board, "Inmate Firefighters Are Helping to Save California. Give Them a Chance at Full-Time Jobs," *Los Angeles Times*, November 1, 2019, www.latimes.com/opinion/story/2019-11-01/california -inmate-firefighters.

19 Thomas Fuller, "Covid Limits California's Efforts to Fight Wildfires with Prison Labor," *New York Times*, August 24, 2020, www.nytimes.com /2020/08/22/us/california-wildfires-prisoners.html.

20 Worth Rises, *The Prison Industrial Complex: Mapping Private Sector Players*, April 2020, https://worthrises.org/theprisonindustry2020.

21 Wendy Sawyer and Peter Wagner, "Mass Incarceration: The Whole Pie 2023," Prison Policy Initiative, March 2023, www.prisonpolicy.org/reports/pie2023.html.

22 Dave Davies, "Surveillance and Local Police: How Technology Is Evolving Faster Than Regulation," NPR, January 27, 2021, www.npr.org/2021/01/27/961103187/surveillance-and-local-police-how-technology-is-evolving-faster-than-regulation.

23 Liz Mineo, "Racial Wealth Gap May Be a Key to Other Inequities," *Harvard Gazette*, June 17, 2021, https://news.harvard.edu/gazette/story/2021/06/racial-wealth-gap-may-be-a-key-to-other-inequities/.

24 Adam Smith, *An Inquiry into the Nature and Causes of the Wealth of Nations* (London, 1776).

25 Fanon, *Black Skin White Masks*, xv.

26 Daniel Costa. "The Farmworker Wage Gap Continued in 2020," Economic Policy Institute, July 20, 2021.

27 Charlie Savage, "Countrywide Will Settle a Bias Suit," *New York Times*, December 21, 2011, www.nytimes.com/2011/12/22/business/us-settlement-reported-on-countrywide-lending.html.

28 Rothstein, *Color of Law*, 152.

29 Rothstein, 158.

30 Rothstein, 130–31.

31 Gilmore, *Golden Gulag*, 130.

32 Gilmore, 174.

Chapter 3: Reimagining Communities: Ivan Kilgore, United Black Family Scholarship Foundation

1 "The 2020 Pulitzer Price Finalists in Audio Reporting," Pulitzer Prizes, 2020, www.pulitzer.org/finalists/nigel-poor-earlonne-woods-and-rahsaan-thomas.

2 Sam Stanton and Wes Venteicher, "Exclusive: FBI Investigating Sacramento Prison Plagued by Inmate Slayings, Hazing," *Sacramento Bee*, May 17, 2021, www.sacbee.com/news/local/article251004399.html.

3 Dan Morain, "1 Inmate Killed, 13 Hurt in Prison Fight," *Los Angeles Times*, March 5, 2019. www.latimes.com/archives/la-xpm-1996-09-28-mn-48282 -story.html; "Inmates Injured in Riot at New Folsom Prison," Associated Press, December 7, 2011.

4 "Hugo Pinell Killed in California Prison; San Quentin 6 Member Slit Guard's Throat in 1971 Escape Attempt," *Mercury News*, August 12, 2015, www.mercurynews.com/2015/08/12/hugo-pinell-killed-in-california -prison-san-quentin-6-member-slit-guards-throat-in-1971-escape-attempt/.

5 "COVID-19 Review Series, Part Three: Transfer of Patients from California Institution for Men," California Office of the Inspector General, February 1, 2021.

6 Femi Redwood, "This Is What It's Like to Be in Prison During Coronavirus," Vice News, April 2, 2020, https://www.youtube.com/watch?v =tynlUWVcUQU.

7 George Jackson, *Soledad Brother: The Prison Letters of George Jackson* (Putnam, 1970), 6.

8 john powell, "Keynote: The Mechanisms of Othering," Othering & Belonging Institute, University of California, Berkeley, May 30, 2015, https://belonging.berkeley.edu/john-powell-keynote-mechanisms -othering.

9 Ivan Kilgore, *Mayhem, Murder & Magnificence: A Memoir* (Self-published, 2020), 16.

10 William Evans, Craig Garthwaite, and Timothy Moore, "Guns and Violence: The Enduring Impact of Crack Cocaine Markets on Young Black Males," NBER Working Paper Series, July 2018.

11 Zach Norris, *Defund Fear: Safety Without Policing, Prisons, and Punishment* (Beacon, 2021), 60.

12 Zusha Elinson, "As Mayor, Brown Remade Oakland's Downtown and Himself," *New York Times*, September 2, 2010, www.nytimes.com/2010/09 /03/us/politics/03bcbrown.html.

13 Rothstein, *Color of Law*, 211.

14 Norris, *Defund Fear,* 48.

15 Mariame Kaba, *We Do This 'Til We Free Us: Abolitionist Organizing and Transforming Justice* (Haymarket, 2021), 14.

16 Kaba, *'Til We Free Us*, 139.

17 Brentin Mock, "What Should Be Done about Rikers Island's Dark Fugitive Slave History?" *Bloomberg*, July 23, 2015, www.bloomberg.com/news/articles/2015-07-23/what-should-be-done-about-rikers-island-s-dark-fugitive-slave-history.

18 James Ridgeway, "America's 10 Worst Prisons: Rikers Island," *Mother Jones*, May 14, 2013, www.motherjones.com/politics/2013/05/america-10-worst-prisons-rikers-island-new-york-city/.

19 Ridgeway, "10 Worst Prisons."

20 Kaba, *'Til We Free Us*, 20.

21 Frederick Douglass, *My Bondage and My Freedom* (Miller, 1855), 153.

Chapter 4: Reimagining Justice: Critical Resistance

1   "The People's Plan for Prison Closure," Californians United for a Responsible Budget (CURB), April 2021, https://curbprisonspending.org/wp-content/uploads/2021/04/Peoples-Plan-for-Prison-Closure.pdf.

2   William McCurry, "Legislative Analyst's Office Skeptical after 'Warm Shutdown' of Deuel Vocational Institution," *Davis Vanguard*, February 9, 2021, www.davisvanguard.org/2021/02/legislative-analysts-office-skeptical-after-warm-shutdown-of-deuel-vocational-institution/.

3   "California Announces First Closure of State Prison Since 2003," CBS News, September 25, 2020, www.cbsnews.com/sacramento/news/california-announces-first-closure-of-state-prison-since-2003/.

4   Tim Arango and Max Whittaker, "'Nothing Will Be the Same': A Prison Town Weighs a Future without a Prison," *New York Times*, January 13, 2022, www.nytimes.com/2022/01/10/us/susanville-california-prison-closing.html.

5   "Dr. Angela Davis: Activist, Educator, and Social Justice Legend," interview by the California Endowment, October 21, 2021, https://www.youtube.com/watch?v=CKnF-Gap1_Q.

6   "Our History," Critical Resistance, n.d., https://criticalresistance.org/mission-vision/history/.

7   Matthew Green, "Packing the House: The Back Story on California's Prison Boom," KQED, January 6, 2012, www.kqed.org/lowdown/457/packing-the-house-how-big-is-californias-prison-system.

8   "Criminal Justice Reform Is Working in California," California Budget and Policy Center, December 21, 2021, https://calbudgetcenter.org/resources/criminal-justice-reform-is-working-in-california/.

9 Gary Stewart, "Black Codes and Broken Windows: The Legacy of Racial Hegemony in Anti-Gang Civil Injunctions," *Yale Law Journal* 107, no. 7 (1998): 2249–79, https://openyls.law.yale.edu/handle/20.500.13051/9095.

10 Eric Arnold, "Oakland Gang Injunctions: Gentrification or Public Safety?," *RP&E Journal* 18, no. 2 (Autumn 2011), www.reimaginerpe.org/18-2/arnold.

11 Frank P. Barajas, "An Invading Army: A Civil Gang Injunction in a Southern California Chicana/O Community," *Latino Studies* 5, no. 4 (December 1, 2007): 393–417, https://doi.org/10.1057/palgrave.lst.8600280.

12 Monte Francis, "Oakland Approves Bratton after 9-Hour Meeting," NBC Bay Area, January 23, 2013, www.nbcbayarea.com/news/local/oakland-approves-bratton-after-9-hour-meeting/1950399/.

13 "We Won! A Full Victory against Gang Injunctions!" Stop the Injunctions in Oakland, February 10, 2017, https://stoptheinjunction.wordpress.com/2017/02/10/we-won-a-full-victory-against-gang-injunctions/.

14 Randal C. Archibold, "Immigrants Take to U.S. Streets in Show of Strength," *New York Times*, May 2, 2006, www.nytimes.com/2006/05/02/us/02immig.html.

15 Mariame Kaba and Eva Nagao, "What about the Rapists?," Abolitionist FAQ Series, Interrupting Criminalization, 2021, www.interruptingcriminalization.com/what-about-the-rapists.

16 T. K. Logan and Roberta Valente, "Who Will Help Me? Domestic Violence Survivors Speak Out about Law Enforcement Responses," National Domestic Violence Hotline, January 28, 2021, https://www.thehotline.org/wp-content/uploads/sites/3/2015/09/NDVH-2015-Law-Enforcement-Survey-Report.pdf.

17 Jon Ortiz, "Prison Officers' Union PAC Collects $8.2 Million from Members," *Sacramento Bee*, February 3, 2016, www.sacbee.com/news/politics-government/the-state-worker/article58052373.html.

18 Gabriel Petek, "The 2023–24 Budget: The California Department of Corrections and Rehabilitation," Legislative Analyst's Office, State of California, February 2023.

19 Yvonne Yen Liu, "Prison Strike's Financial Impact in California," Solidarity Research Center, October 2016, http://solidarityresearch.org/project/prison-strikes-financial-impact-california/.

20 "Prison Labor in California State Prisons," Investigate: A Project of the American Friends Service Committee, n.d., https://investigate.afsc.org/prison-labor-california-state-prisons.

21 Matthew Mitchell, "California Occupational Licensing: Barriers to Opportunity in the Golden State," Mercatus Center, August 13, 2019, www.mercatus.org/research/state-testimonies/california-occupational-licensing-barriers-opportunity-golden-state.

22 Angela Y. Davis, *Are Prisons Obsolete?* (Seven Stories, 2011), 12.

23 Davis, *Are Prisons Obsolete?*, 50.

24 Norris, *Defund Fear*, 3.

25 Petek, "2023–24 Budget."

26 Petek.

27 Nigel Duara, "Gavin Newsom Moved to Close 4 California Prisons. How Many More Can He Shut?" CalMatters, February 22, 2023, https://calmatters.org/justice/2023/02/how-many-prisons-does-california-need/.

28 Hailey Branson-Potts, "A Rural California Town Sued to Keep a Prison Open. Judge Rules Newsom Can Close It," *Los Angeles Times*, September 13, 2022, www.latimes.com/california/story/2022-09-09/la-me-rural-california-prison-closure-lawsuit.

29 "Planned Closure of Chuckawalla Valley State Prison," California Department of Corrections and Rehabilitation, press release, December 6, 2022, www.cdcr.ca.gov/news/2022/12/06/california-department-of-corrections-and-rehabilitation-announces-the-planned-closure-of-chuckawalla-valley-state-prison/.

30 "Prison Closure Roadmap," Californians United for a Responsible Budget (CURB), February 2023, https://curbprisonspending.org/wp-content/uploads/2023/03/FILE_7463.pdf.

31 Kaba, *'Til We Free Us*, 62.

Chapter 5: Reimagining Capitalism: Greenwood

1 A. R. Shaw, "Raphael Warnock Joins D-Nice, Killer Mike For 'Shop Talk' ahead of Election Day," *Atlanta Daily World*, December 7, 2022, https://atlantadailyworld.com/2022/12/06/raphael-warnock-joins-d-nice-killer-mike-for-shop-talk-ahead-of-election-day/.

2 Matt Walljasper, "The Rebirth of Bankhead Seafood," *Atlanta Magazine,* September 19, 2022, www.atlantamagazine.com/news-culture-articles/the-rebirth-of-bankhead-seafood/.

3 Donovan X. Ramsey and Christian Cody, "The Political Education of Killer Mike," *GQ*, July 8, 2020, www.gq.com/story/killer-mike-the -atlanta-way.

4 "Killer Mike's Economic Solution for the Black Community," MTV, July 8, 2016, www.mtv.com/movie-and-tv-awards/video-clips/41huod /killer-mike-s-economic-solution-for-the-black-community.

5 Haisten Willis, "Nearly 100 Years Old, Black-Owned Citizens Trust Bank Champions Homeownership, Development," *Atlanta Journal-Constitution,* February 18, 2020, www.ajc.com/business/committed-the -community/vxca8AuhxALRadmZJ5UyfN/.

6 Marielle Segarra, "The Bank Black Movement Gains Traction," *Marketplace*, April 29, 2019, www.marketplace.org/2017/04/20/bank-black -movement-gains-traction/.

7 Segarra, "Bank Black Movement."

8 "Consider This: Bounce TV," WMBF News, September 27, 2011, www .wmbfnews.com/story/15557538/consider-this-bounce-tv/.

9 Rothstein, *Color of Law*, 185.

10 "About Us," Greenwood, n.d., https://gogreenwood.com/about/.

11 "Fintech Startup Greenwood Raises $40 Million in Funding to Provide Black and Latino Banking Services," press release, Greenwood, March 25, 2021, https://gogreenwood.com/press-release/fintech-startup-greenwood -raises-40-million-in-funding-to-provide-black-and-latino-banking -services/.

12 "Greenwood Studios," Greenwood, n.d., https://gogreenwood.com /greenwood-studio/.

13 "Angela Davis: We Can't Eradicate Racism without Eradicating Racial Capitalism," *Democracy Now!*, June 14, 2020, www.youtube.com/watch?v =qhh3CMkngkY.

14 Maggie Anderson, *Our Black Year: One Family's Quest to Buy Black in America's Racially Divided Economy*, Public Affairs, 2012; "Circulation of Dollars in Black Communities," Black Star Project, October 8, 2022, www.blackstarproject.org/index.php/advocacy-organizing/circulate -black-dollars-in-black-community.html.

15 "Greenwood District," Oklahoma Historical Society, n.d., www.okhistory .org/publications/enc/entry.php?entry=GR024.

16 Dr. Martin Luther King Jr., *Letter from the Birmingham Jail* (Harper-Collins, 1994).

17 "Atlanta Olympics: By the Numbers," *Sports Business Journal*, July 18, 2016, www.sportsbusinessjournal.com/Journal/Issues/2016/07/18/Olympics/Atlanta-by-the-numbers.aspx.

18 "College Enrollment Rates," National Center for Education Statistics, updated May 2023, https://nces.ed.gov/programs/coe/indicator/cpb/college-enrollment-rate.

19 "Greenwood, Inc. Acquires Valence to Provide Professional Development and Job Recruiting for the Black Community," press release, Greenwood, June 22, 2022, https://gogreenwood.com/press-release/valence/.

20 "Greenwood and Travis Hunter Sign NIL Deal and Partner to Launch the 'Choose Black' Campaign," press release, Greenwood, June 27, 2027, https://gogreenwood.com/travishunter/.

21 Sophie Caraan, "Killer Mike Reintroduces Himself in 'MICHAEL,'" Hypebeast, June 16, 2023, https://hypebeast.com/2023/6/killer-mike-michael-album-stream.

22 United Press International, "Young Easily Wins Again in Atlanta," *Chicago Tribune*, August 9, 2021, www.chicagotribune.com/news/ct-xpm-1985-10-10-8503090318-story.html.

23 Rothstein, *Color of Law*, 46.

24 Zachary Hansen, "How Many Fortune 500 Companies Does Atlanta Have?" *Atlanta Journal-Constitution*, June 16, 2023.

25 Yuliya Parshina-Kottas, Anjali Singhvi, Audra D. S. Burch, Troy Griggs, Mika Gröndahl, Lingdong Huang, Tim Wallace, Jeremy White, and Josh Williams, "What the 1921 Tulsa Race Massacre Destroyed," *New York Times*, November 15, 2021, www.nytimes.com/interactive/2021/05/24/us/tulsa-race-massacre.html.

Chapter 6: Reimagining Infrastructure: The Autonomous Infrastructure Mission (AIM)

1 Fanon, *Black Skin, White Masks*, xi.

2 Molly Crabapple and Michael K. Williams, "The Zo, Videos about Prison Life," Marshall Project, February 27, 2020, www.themarshallproject.org/2020/02/27/welcome-to-the-zo.

3 "Heshima Speaks about the Amend the 13th Movement," Amend the 13th, August 19, 2017, www.youtube.com/watch?v=ByWc8GerU1U.

4 Hô Chí Minh, *On Revolution. Selected Writings, 1920–1966*, 1968.

5   Heshima Denham, "On the Correlation between the Autonomous Infra-structure Mission and George Jackson's 'On Withdrawal,'" January 2023.

6   Benjamin Wallace-Wells, "The Plot from Solitary," *New York Magazine*, April 11, 2019, https://nymag.com/news/features/solitary-secure -housing-units-2014-2/.

7   Gabrielle Canon, "Ending Inmate Isolation: Inside the Battle to Stop Sol-itary Confinement in America," Medium, June 21, 2016, https://medium .com/@gabriellecanon/ending-solitary-confinement-bb4e031e058.

8   Wallace-Wells, "Plot from Solitary."

9   "United States: Prolonged Solitary Confinement Amounts to Psychologi-cal Torture, Says UN Expert," UN Human Rights Council, Special Proce-dures, press release, February 28, 2020.

10 Wallace-Wells, "Plot from Solitary."

11 *Ashker v. Governor of California,* 09-cv-05796 CW.

12 "What Is the Foster Care-to-Prison Pipeline?," Juvenile Law Center, May 26, 2018, https://jlc.org/news/what-foster-care-prison-pipeline.

13 Rothstein, *Color of Law*, 96.

14 Rothstein, 95–96.

15 Mackenzi Huyser and Judi Ravenhorst Meerman, "Resident Perceptions of Redevelopment and Gentrification in the Heartside Neighborhood: Lessons for the Social Work Profession," *Journal of Sociology & Social Welfare* 41, no. 3 (2014), https://scholarworks.wmich.edu/jssw/vol41/iss3/2/.

16 "Baxter Demographics and Statistics," Niche, n.d., https://www.niche .com/places-to-live/n/baxter-grand-rapids-mi/residents/.

17 Megan Burks, Christine T. Nguyen, and Evan Frost, "Six Months in, the Call for Justice at 38th and Chicago Persists," MPR News, December 3, 2020, https://www.mprnews.org/story/2020/11/25/timeline-building -george-floyd-square.

18 Mao Zedong, *On Contradiction*, April 1937.

19 J. Heshima Denham, "A Day in the Life of an Imprisoned Revolution-ary," *San Francisco Bay View*, May 8, 2012.

Chapter 7: Conclusion: Beyond Freedom

1   "What Happened during Egypt's January 25 Revolution?," Al Jazeera, Jan-uary 25, 2023, www.aljazeera.com/news/2023/1/25/what-happened-during -egypts-january-25-revolution.

2 "Ten Years Later: Reflections on Egypt's 2011 Uprising," Arab Center Washington DC, February 19, 2021, https://arabcenterdc.org/resource/ten-years-later-reflections-on-egypts-2011-uprising/.

3 Alexander, *New Jim Crow*, 223.

4 Ed Pilkington, "Fears of Renewed FBI Abuse of Power after Informant Infiltrated BLM Protests," *Guardian*, February 14, 2023, https://www.theguardian.com/us-news/2023/feb/14/fbi-abuse-of-power-alleged-informant-denver-blm-protests.

5 Angela Davis, "Living the Legacy: The 58th Commemoration of El-Hajj Malik El-Shabazz – Malcolm X," Malcolm X & Dr. Betty Shabaaz Memorial & Education Center, February 21, 2023.

6 Jackson, *Blood in My Eye*, 86–87.

7 Angela Davis and Elizabeth Martínez, "Building Coalitions of People of Color," interview by University of California, San Diego, panel discussion, May 12, 1993.

8 Elizabeth Sutherland Martínez, *De Colores Means All of Us: Latina Views for a Multi-Colored Century* (South End, 1998).

9 "15 Facts about Latino Well-Being in CA," Latino Policy & Politics Institute, October 26, 2022, https://latino.ucla.edu/research/15-facts-latinos-california/.

10 Mark Twain, *The Mysterious Stranger and Other Stories* (Harper & Brothers, 1916), 247–48.

11 Rick Rouan, "Fact Check: Missing Context in Claim about Black Lives Matter Co-Founder's Property Purchases," *USA Today*, April 26, 2021, www.usatoday.com/story/news/factcheck/2021/04/19/fact-check-misleading-claim-blm-co-founders-real-estate/7241450002/.

12 Elan Hope, "Rethinking Civic Engagement," Brennan Center for Justice, February 16, 2022, www.brennancenter.org/our-work/research-reports/rethinking-civic-engagement.

13 Maiysha Kai, "Unapologetic: Activist and Author Charlene Carruthers Says Radical Movements Require Radical Honesty," *The Root*, September 2, 2018, www.theroot.com/unapologetic-activist-and-author-charlene-carruthers-s-1828670627.

14 "CEO, ASJ; National Director, TimeDone," Alliance for Safety and Justice, June 14, 2022, https://allianceforsafetyandjustice.org/staff/ceo/.

15 Alliance for Safety and Justice, *Crime Survivors Speak*, 2022, https://
    allianceforsafetyandjustice.org/wp-content/uploads/2022/09/Alliance
    -for-Safety-and-Justice-Crime-Survivors-Speak-September-2022.pdf.

16 Jay Jordan, "Life after Incarceration," *The Problem with Jon Stewart*,
    May 24, 2023.

Glossary

1 Jacob Rosenberg, "'Love It or Leave It' Has a Racist History. A Lot of
   America's Language Does," *Mother Jones*, July 20, 2019, www.motherjones
   .com/politics/2019/07/love-it-or-leave-it-has-a-racist-history-a-lot-of
   -americas-language-does/.

2 Elisabeth McLean, "What Are Ban the Box Laws?" Goodhire, August 28,
   2020, www.goodhire.com/blog/ban-the-box/.

3 Combahee River Collective, "The Combahee River Collective: A Black
   Feminist Statement," in *Capitalist Patriarchy and the Case for Socialist Feminism*, ed. Zillah R. Eisenstein (Monthly Review Press, 1978), 362–72.

4 Emma Anderson, "The Evolution of Electronic Monitoring Devices,"
   NPR, May 24, 2014.

5 "Global GPS Market and Its Applications," Markets and Markets, 2023,
   www.marketsandmarkets.com/Market-Reports/global-GPS-market-and
   -its-applications-142.html.

6 "Fast Facts: Historically Black Colleges and Universities (667)," National
   Center for Education Statistics, n.d., https://nces.ed.gov/fastfacts/display
   .asp?id=667.

7 "School-to-Prison Pipeline," American Civil Liberties Union, February 15, 2022.

8 Lisa Stolzenberg and Stewart J. D'Alessio, "'Three Strikes and You're
   Out': The Impact of California's New Mandatory Sentencing Law on
   Serious Crime Rates," *Crime & Delinquency* 43, no. 4 (October 1, 1997):
   457–69.

Index

A

abolition
    capitalism and, 86
    as constructive practice, 75–77
    by default, 74–75
    definition of, 5
    as historical movement, 4–5
    modern concept of, 4–5
    object of, 20
accountability, 143
activism
    components of, 81
    current landscape for, 125
    self-care and, 129–130
    strategies for, 125–130
Adler, Stella, xvi
Agbebiyi, K, 134
agency, 40–45
Ahrens, Lois, xx
Alexander, Michelle, xxi, 14, 124, 145
Alliance for Safety and Justice, 135–136
All of Us or None, xvi, xxii–xxiii,
    xxviii–xxx, xxxiii, 3, 4, 64, 73, 102,
    126, 128–129
ally, definition of, 143
Alter, Jonathan, 92
Amazon, 24
Amend the 13th, 102, 108, 109–110
American Civil Liberties Union, 35, 66, 151
Amuchie, Nnennaya, 134
Anderson, William, 44
Angola State Prison, xxxiii, xxxviii
Anthony, Susan B., xxxix
Anticipation, xix, xlii

Anti-Recidivism Coalition, 10
antisemitism, 127, 143
Aristotle, xxii
Armstrong, Greg, 38
art
    incarcerated individuals and,
        xvi–xvii, xxv–xxvi
    key elements of, xvii
    power of, xv–xvi
Arts in Corrections, xvi
Aryan Brotherhood, 35, 106
Ashker, Todd, 106
Aspiration, 84
assimilation, xxxiii–xxxiv, 143–144
Atlanta
    Black youth in, 89–90
    Collier Heights, 87–88
    HBCUs in, 90
    Olympic Games, 93–94
    protests in, 95
    sports teams, 80
Autonomous Infrastructure Mission
    (AIM), 106–111, 114–121
Avenal State Prison, 60

B

Bacon, Nathaniel, 19
Bacon's Rebellion, 19, 20, 140
bail, 8–9
Baldwin, James, xxxii
bandele, asha, 132
#BankBlack movement, 81, 82, 85, 88
Bankhead Seafood, 80
banking system, 82–85

Bank of America, 26, 82, 85
Ban the Box, 3, 135, 144
Berkeley, William, 19
BET News, 81
Biden, Joe, 137–138
Bigger Than Life, xxiii, 78
Birts, Ali, 1–4, 8, 74
Black Americans. *See also* racism; slavery
    assimilation and, xxxiii–xxxiv
    buying power of, 97–98
    under correctional control, 5
    disenfranchisement and, xxx, xxxv,
        xxxviii, 5, 136, 138
    racial wealth gap and, 24–26, 83
    violence against, 5, 140
Black Codes, xxxviii, 23
Black feminism, 144
Black Guerrilla Family, 105, 106
Black Liberation Army, 88
Black Lives Matter, 125, 131–132, 144
Black Panther Party, 45, 53, 88, 110, 111, 116,
    121, 144–145
Black Skin, White Masks, xxxiii
Black Wall Street, 86–92, 97, 120
Black Youth Project 100 (BYP100),
    132–133
blockbusting, 112
Blood in My Eye, 19, 104
Bloody Sunday, 140
Bloomberg, Michael, 138
Booker, Cory, 138
Borgeson, Isa, 61–63, 70
Boudin, Chesa, 8–12, 64
Bounce TV, 83
Brashere, Adam, 108–110, 114
Bratton, Bill, 66
Braz, Rose, 57
brokenness, 45–50
Brown, Jerry, 43
Brown, Mike, 108
Budnick, Scott, 10
Buttigieg, Pete, 138
BYP100 (Black Youth Project 100), 132–133

C

California Arts in Corrections, xvi
California Correctional Center, 60, 63,
    76–77

California Correctional Institution, 60
California Correctional Peace Officers
    Association (CCPOA), 70, 71
California Institution for Men, 36
California Medical Facility, 60
California Men's Colony, 60
Californians United for a Responsible
    Budget (CURB), 60, 61, 77
California Prison Industry Authority, 73
California Rehabilitation Center, 60
California State Prison Los Angeles
    County, 60
California State Prison Sacramento. *See*
    New Folsom prison
California State Prison Solano, 33, 34, 37
California Substance Abuse Treatment
    Facility, 60
Campaign Zero, 133
capitalism. *See also* Greenwood
    abolition and, 86
    concept of, 25
    engaging with, 93–95
    inequality and, 26
    slavery and, 25, 26, 86
Carruthers, Charlene, 133
Carter, Jimmy, 92
Castellanos, Arturo, 106
Castile, Philando, 82
Castro Julián, 138
Charlamagne tha God, 82
Chauvin, Derek, xxix
Chime, 84
Chuckawalla Valley State Prison, 60
Cimarron City Correctional Facility, 40
Citizens Trust, 82
civil disobedience, 145
Civil Rights Act of 1964, 91, 140
Clark Atlanta University, 90
Close California Prisons coalition, 60,
    67, 68
Closed-Circuit Economic Initiative, 109
CLOSErikers, 46
Coastal Community Bank, 84
Cohen, Cathy, 133
COINTELPRO, 117, 125, 145
colorblind racism, 145
The Color of Law, 21
Combahee River Collective, 133, 144

community. *See also* REBUILD program;
 United Black Family Scholarship
 Foundation
  boundaries defining, 21–22
  race and, 21–22
  social control and, 21–22
Community Safe-Zones Initiative, 109,
 115–118
Congress for Racial Equality, 146
co-opting, xxxvi
Countrywide Financial, 26–27
COVID Creature, xxii
COVID pandemic
  approaches to, 7–8
  demonstrations during, xxx
  prison labor and, 24
  in prisons, 36–37
  vaccines and, 8
crack epidemic, 39–40
Crime Survivors Speak, 136
criminal, definition of, xxxix–xl
criminalization, xxxviii, 145
criminal justice system. *See also*
 incarceration; prisons
  fantasy of reforming from within, 11–12
  racism as foundational to, xxxviii
  technology and, 8
Critical Resistance (CR), 57–62, 64–68,
 72, 75
Cullors, Patrisse, 132
cultural racism, 146

D

Daniels, Isaiah, xix
Davis, Angela, 57, 63–64, 74–75, 86, 125, 128
Day-Lewis, Daniel, xv
Day Without an Immigrant, 68
Defund Fear, 43, 75
"Defund the Police," 133–134, 146
Denham, Dudley, 111, 113
Denham, Duvon, 111–112, 113
Denham, Heshima, xxxvi, 101–108,
 110–115, 117–121
Deuel Vocational Institution, 60, 61, 76
directly impacted, definition of, 146
disenfranchisement, xxx, xxxv, xxxviii,
 5, 136, 138
Disney, 6

Doing Time, xviii, xix, 100
Domestic Genocide, xxxv, 41, 46
Doolittle, Patrick, 102
Dorsainvil, Rianka R., 85
Douglass, Frederick, 48, 50
Dream Corps, 10
Dru, Eli, 134
Ducart, Clark, 104

E

Ear Hustle, 35
Edmund Pettus Bridge, 140
Education for Liberation Coalition, 59
Egyptian revolution of 2011, 123–124
Ehrlichman, John, 18
8 Can't Wait, 133–134
8toAbolition, 133–135
Ella Baker Center for Human Rights,
 42–43
el-Sisi, Abdel Fattah, 124
Emergency Response Network, 109
equity, definition of, 146
Ervin, Woods, 59, 67–70, 131
E. W. Scripps Company, 83

F

Fairchild, Henry Pratt, 20
Families United, 108
Fanon, Frantz, xxxii, xxxiii–xxxiv, 17, 25,
 58, 101, 110, 114
FBI, xxxix, 35, 48, 125, 129, 145
Federal Housing Authority, 21, 112
Floyd, George, xviii, xxviii, xxix, 58, 108,
 116, 128, 132
food deserts, 22, 28
food stability, 115
The Fountainhead, 25
Fowler, Bruce, xix
Foxx, Kim, 9
Francis, Chris, 71
freedom, concept of, 123–124, 139
Freedom Fridays, 58–59
Free Speech Movement, 45, 146–147

G

Gandhi, Mohandas, xxxix
gang injunctions, 65–67
Garvey, Marcus, xxi, 38

Garza, Alicia, 132
Gascón, George, 11
Gathering Spot, 95–96
Geidner, Chris, 10
GEM Trainers, 46
gentrification, 43–44, 65–66, 67, 82, 114
Gilmore, Ruth Wilson, 22, 23, 28, 29, 57
Global Tel Link, 74
Glover, Ryan, 83–85, 96, 98
GPS monitoring, 74, 147
grassroots movements, 147
Great American Boycott, 68
Greenbook, 85–86
Greenwood (digital bank), 81, 84–86, 88, 90, 92–97
Greenwood (Tulsa district), 86–88, 97
Greenwood Studios, 85
Griffin-Gracy, Miss Major, 68
Guillen, Antonio, 106
Gurley, O. W., 87

H

Hamid, Sarah T., 134
Hampton, Fred, 110, 125, 145
Hanway, Jonas, 22–23, 74
Harari, Yuval Noah, 127
Harney, Stefano, 20
Harris, Kamala, 138
Hawkins, Bri, 107–110, 114–118
HBCUs (historically Black colleges and universities), 90, 96, 98, 147
Herskind, Micah, 134
High Desert State Prison, 63
historical trauma, 147
Hollie, Jessica, 66
Hoover, J. Edgar, 48
horizontal prejudice, 28, 125, 147
hot-spot policing, xxxi, 65, 148
Howard, Curtis, 73
Human Rights Watch, 35
Humans of San Quentin, xviii
Hunnicutt, Carnell, Sr., xvii, xx–xxii, xxv, xxxvi, 16
Hunter, Travis, 96
Hurricane Katrina, 67

I

identity politics, 13, 134

immigration, 19–20, 68, 127, 129
incarceration. *See also* prisons
    alternatives to, 5–6, 64–65, 75–77, 135–136
    experiences of, xviii–xix, xxi, xxxii–xxxiii, 2–3, 33–37, 102–107
    increase in, 149
    rate of, by country, 5, 103
    resilience and, 51
    school-to-prison pipeline, 151
    solitary confinement, 104, 105–106, 120–121
Indigenous people, displacement of, 19, 37, 103
infiltration, 117, 125, 145
infrastructure. *See also* Autonomous Infrastructure Mission
    accessibility and, 28
    definition of, 28
    interstate highway system, 27–28
    racism and, 28–29

institutional racism, 18, 148
Interrupting Criminalization, 68, 69
interstate highway system, 27–28

J

Jackson, George, xxxii, 19, 35, 38, 97, 110–111, 114, 126
Jackson, Jesse, 111
Jackson, Maynard, 87
Jackson State University, 96
Jailhouse Lawyers Speak, 108
Jamaa, Sitawa, 106
January 6 riot, 13–14
Jim Crow laws, 83, 148
Johnson, Alice, 88–89
Johnson, Connie, 46
Johnson, Edward, 88–89
Jones, Sabrina, xx, xxxvi
Jones, Van, 10
Jordan, Jay, 135–136
justice. *See also* criminal justice system; Critical Resistance
    definition of, 30
    racial, 150
    restorative, 119, 151
    social, 151

Justice Arts Coalition, xvi
Justice Collaborative, 10
Just Mercy, 10

K

Kaba, Mariame, 48–49, 50, 68, 77
Kandinsky, Wassily, xxiv
Kendi, Ibram X., 144
Kern Valley State Prison, 60, 101–102, 107
Khalil, Noel, 80
Kilgore, Ivan, xxxv, xxxvi, 33–48, 50–55, 102, 126
Killer Mike (Mike Render), 79–84, 86–89, 94–99
Kim, Jennifer, 71
King, Coretta Scott, 93
King, Martin Luther, Jr., xii, xxiii, xxxix, 14, 88, 89, 90–91, 92, 94, 95, 97, 98, 125, 145
King Center for Nonviolent Social Change, 84
King: The Early Years, xxxv
Kleiner, Morris, 73
Klobuchar, Amy, 138
Kochiyama, Yuri, xxxix
Krasner, Larry, 9
Ku Klux Klan, 63, 103
Kuo, Rachel, 134

L

Langston University, 47
laughter, as self-care, 129–130
Legal Services for Prisoners with Children (LSPC), xxxiii, 3–4
Lessons in Liberation, 59
"Letter from the Birmingham Jail," 91
Lewis, John, xxiii, 140
LGBTQ (LGBTQIA+), definition of, 148
Light, Ken and Melanie, xxx
Locke, John, 23
Loftus, Suzy, 10

M

Malcolm X, xi–xiii, xxi, xxxix, 34, 48, 98, 125, 145
Mandela, Nelson, xxxix
Mao Zedong, 114, 121
Marcos, Ferdinand, 61
marginalized, definition of, 148–149

Marshall Project, 102, 135
Martin, Glenn E., xxxv, 46, 51, 54
Martin, Trayvon, 131
Martínez, Elizabeth, 128
mass incarceration, definition of, 149
Mathew, Viju, 61, 63, 70, 76
Mauer, Marc, xx, xxi, xxxv–xxxvi
Mayhem, Murder & Magnificence, xxxv, 38
McKinney, Cynthia and James, 87
McNamara, Megan, 46
Merts, Peter, xxv
Mexican Mafia, 106
Microsoft, 24
Millions for Prisoners March, 102
Minsker, Natasha, 70
Mitchell, Matthew, 73
Moderna, 8
Mohapatra, Mon, 134
Moody, Robert F., 76
Morehouse College, 90
Morgan, Gerald, xvii, xviii–xix, xxv, xlii, 56, 100
Morris Brown College, 90
Morsi, Mohamed, 124
Moten, Fred, 20
movement building, 149
Movement for Black Lives, 131–132
MTV News, 81
Mubarak, Hosni, 123
Murray, George M., 91
My Comrades' Thoughts on Black Lives Matter, xxxv

N

NAACP (National Association for the Advancement of Colored People), 84
National Negro Congress, 63
Nation of Islam, 88
New Afrikan Math and Science Centers Initiative, 109
New Afrikan Revolutionary Nationalists, 104, 114
New Deal, 27
New Folsom prison, 34, 35, 52
The New Jim Crow, xxi, 14, 124, 145
Newsom, Gavin, 70
Nixon, Richard, 18, 23
No New SF Jails, 68

Norris, Zach, 42–43, 44, 75
North Kern State Prison, 60
Not Feeling the Freedom, xxiii, 32
Nuestra Familia, 106
Nunn, Dorsey, 3, 4, 126, 129

O

Obama, Barack, 64, 140
Old Folsom prison, 2
Oliver, Ken, xxxi–xxxiv, xxxviii, 128
Olympic Games, 93–94
O'Neil, Caitlin, 76
O'Neil, Stephen E., xxxii
Operation PUSH (People United to
    Serve Humanity), 111
oppression, systems of, 30–31
Oppression Olympics, 128–129
O'Rourke, Beto, 138
othering, 38, 44
Owens, Jesse, 93

P

Payne, Billy, 93–94
Pelican Bay State Prison, xxxiii, 104, 105
people of color, definition of, 149
The People's Plan for Prison Closure, 60
Pfizer, 8
Picturing Resistance, xxx
Pierce, Sahirenys, 85
Pinell, Hugo, 35
Pink Floyd, xxiii
Pleasant Valley State Prison, 60
police officers
    qualified immunity doctrine,
        xxx–xxxi
    race of, 22
police violence
    cause of, xxix–xxx, 48
    deaths and, xxix, xxxi, 6, 12, 81–82,
        108, 125, 128–129, 140
    protests against, xxx–xxxi, 6, 108,
        132–133
policing, hot-spot, xxxi, 65, 148
politics, 136–138
powell, john a., 38
power
    definition of, 149–150
    race and, 19–20

Pressley, Ayanna, 131
pretrial risk assessment tools, 8–9
Prison Journalism Project, xxiii
prison labor, xxix, xxxviii, 5, 23–24, 72–74
Prison Policy Initiative, 135
prisons. *See also* incarceration; *individual
    prisons*
    changing purpose of, 22–23
    closing, 60–61, 70–72, 75–76
    control and, 23, 29, 35, 104–105, 120
    as deterrence, 23
    environmental impact of, 61
    gangs and, 104–105
    growth of, 24, 29, 64
    history of, 22–23
    "invisibility" of, 49–50
    jails vs., xxxviii–xxxix
    local economy and, 62–63
Project NIA, 48
Project ReMADE, 3
punishment. *See also* incarceration;
    prisons
    AIM and, 119–120
    rehabilitation vs., 23, 35, 60
Purnell, Derecka, 134
The Purpose of Power, 132

Q

qualified immunity doctrine, xxx–xxxi
Quetzal Education Consulting, 59

R

race
    community and, 21–22
    othering and, 38
    of police officers, 22
    power and, 19–20
    as social construct, xxvii, 19–20, 150
Race to Incarcerate, xvii, xx, xxi,
    xxxv–xxxvi, 16
racial justice, 150
racial wealth gap, 24–26, 83, 150
racism
    colorblind, 145
    criminal legal system and, xxxviii
    cultural, 146
    economy and, 24–27, 86
    infrastructure and, 28–29

institutional, 18, 148
structural/systemic, xxix, xxxviii, 63, 151–152
radicalization, 2, 38, 62, 63, 67, 88, 108
Rand, Ayn, 25
rape, 69–70
Raven, Leila, 134
Reagan, Ronald, 18
Real Cost of Prisons Project, xx
REBUILD (Reinvest in Every Black and Underserved Institution to Liberate and Diversify) program, 42, 44–47
Reconstruction Era, 23, 150–151
redlining, 83, 85
Reese, Preston, 39
rehabilitation vs. punishment, 23, 35, 60
Render, Mike. See Killer Mike
resilience, 51
restorative justice, 119, 151
revolution
    definition of, 13
    necessity of, 14
    as story of America, 140
Riker, Richard, 48
Rikers Island prison, 46, 49
Ritchie, Andrea J., 68
Robinson, Christopher, 49
Rodin, Auguste, xvii
Rothstein, Richard, 21, 27, 112
Run the Jewels, 80
Russell, Herman, 86, 87
Russo, John, 65–66

S

Salinas Valley State Prison, 34, 41, 45–46
Sam, Tanya, 85
Sanders, Bernie, 137–138
San Francisco Bay View, 102, 121
San Quentin prison, xviii, 34–36
Santa Monica Freeway, 27
Santa Rita Jail, 4
Sapiens, 127
school-to-prison pipeline, 151
Secure Communities Mandate, 109, 116–117
See the Light in Black and White, xv
segregation, 21
self-care, 129–130
self-interest, 25–27

self-liberation, 106, 108, 110, 136–141
Self Portrait (Scott Smith), xiv, xxiv
Seminole County Jail, 40
Sentencing Project, xxxv, 135
sexual assault, 69–70
Shabazz, Betty, xii
Shehk, Mohamed, 58
Show Up for Racial Justice (SURJ), 70
Shrine of the Black Madonna, 87
Shuttlesworth, Fred, 90–91
Sister, 56
slavery, xxix, xxxiii, 25, 26
Small, Delrawn, 82
Smith, Adam, 25–26, 139
Smith, Scott W. (Scotty Scott), xiv, xvii, xxii–xxiv, xxv, 32, 78, 122
social justice, 151
Solano State Prison. See California State Prison Solano
solitary confinement, 104, 105, 120–121
Southern Christian Leadership Conference, 88, 90–91, 95
Southern Negro Youth Congress, 63
Spelman College, 90
Stanford Law School, 3
Steadman, Ralph, xxii
Steele, Carrie, 81
Steinem, Gloria, xxxix
Sterling, Alton, 82
Stevenson, Bryan, 10
Stewart, Gary, 65
Steyer, Tom, 138
Stony Brook University, xxxvi, 46–47, 129
Stop Killing Us protest, xxxi, xxxiv, 128–129
Stop the Injunctions Coalition (STIC), 66–67
Strategic Release Initiative, 109
structural racism, 151–152
Student Nonviolent Coordinating Committee, 133, 146
Sultan, Reina, 134
surveillance, definition of, 152
Sustainable Agricultural Commune, 109, 115
SWAG Shop, 79–80
systemic racism, xxix, xxxviii, 151–152
system impacted, definition of, 152

T

Taylor, Breonna, 128, 132
10K Plan, 43–44
Tharp, Twyla, xx
13th Amendment, xxix, 75, 102, 110. *See also* Amend the 13th
Thomas, Clarence, 23
3M, 24
Three Strikes law, xxxii, xxxiii, 2, 131, 152
T. I., 80
#TimeDone campaign, 135–136
Tlaib, Rashida, 131
Tometi, Ayọ, 132
Transgender Gender Variant Intersex Justice Project, 68
Trump, Donald, 144
Tulsa Race Massacre, 97

U

underground economy, 107–108, 113
United Black Family Scholarship Foundation (UBFSF), 34, 40–42, 46, 47, 53
United Negro College Fund, 84
University of California
    Berkeley, 46
    Irvine, 46, 47
    Santa Cruz, 46

V

Valence, 96
van Gogh, Vincent, xvii
Varo, 84
ViaPath Technologies, 74
Vice News, 36, 37
Vorotnikov, Evgeny, 73
Voting Rights Act of 1965, xxx

W

Walker, Alice, 90
Walker, Madam C. J., 86
Warnock, Raphael G., 79
War on Drugs, 18, 23, 26, 149
wealth
    inequality in, 24–26, 83, 150
    morality and, 26
The Wealth of Nations, 25
We Do This 'Til We Free Us, 77
Wells Fargo, 82, 85
Welsing, Frances Cress, 114
Western Union, 24
When They Call You a Terrorist, 132
whiteness, construction of, 20
Whitten, Robert, 97
Wilson, Ryan, 95
Winfrey, Oprah, 86
Woods, Earlonne, 35
Woods, Mario, 11
word choice, importance of, xxxvii–xxxix
The World Right Now, xxiii, 122
World War II, 21

Y

Yang, Andrew, 138
Young, Andrew, 83–84, 89–94, 96–99
Young, Jean Childs, 89
Youth Community Action Program, 109, 118

Z

The Zo, 102
zoning, 21–22

About the Author

PAULA LEHMAN-EWING is an award-winning journalist and social documentarian. Her work exposing atrocities within the criminal justice system has earned her badges of notoriety from industry leaders and access to the inner workings of the modern civil rights movement.

In 2019 the California Newspaper Publishers Association named Paula a finalist in the category of in-depth reporting for an investigation into Los Angeles's use of pretrial risk assessment tools. The article was the result of a California Public Records Act request and found that the Los Angeles Probation Department was using a faulty tool that categorized most pretrial detainees as high risk. This exposé led to an investigation by the county.

Paula served a transitional role as the communications manager for San Francisco District Attorney Chesa Boudin during his first thirty days in office before she joined the nonprofit Legal Services for Prisoners with Children. At LSPC she launched a publication documenting the personal stories of those directly impacted by the injustices of the criminal legal system. The All of Us or None newspaper is now sent to every prison in California and to more than 160 prison yards across the country. For her work on the paper, Paula was awarded the 2021 Silver Heart from the Society of Professional Journalists for "extraordinary dedication to amplifying the unheard voices of formerly and currently incarcerated people."

Paula continues to work collaboratively with the incarcerated population, serving as a mentor for PEN America and building a digital archive of incarcerated work for Stony Brook University.

Paula has authored articles in mainstream media publications including *BusinessWeek,* Reuters, *Forbes,* Bleacher Report, and *Fortune.* She's contributed to local outlets including the *Daily Journal* (California's largest legal trade publication), the *Daily Breeze* (Hermosa Beach), *East Bay Express* (Oakland), and the *Independently Weekly* (Durham). She holds a master's in journalism from UC Berkeley's Graduate School of Journalism and earned her undergraduate degree from Duke University.

About North Atlantic Books

North Atlantic Books (NAB) is an independent, nonprofit publisher committed to a bold exploration of the relationships between mind, body, spirit, and nature. Founded in 1974, NAB aims to nurture a holistic view of the arts, sciences, humanities, and healing. To make a donation or to learn more about our books, authors, events, and newsletter, please visit www.northatlanticbooks.com.